THE BLACK AMERICAN HANDBOOK
FOR SURVIVAL *THROUGH THE 21ST CENTURY*

VOL. I
The Forgotten Truth Behind Racism in America

THE HIDDEN ANCESTRAL IDENTITY
OF THE BLACK AMERICAN
"WHY IT'S A MATTER OF COLOR"

This is a "Must Have" Book For Every "Black American Family"

The Black American Handbook For Survival Through the 21st Century – Volume I

Rev. Ra Dine Amen-ra

**Quantum Leap Spiritual Life Center Publications
Atlanta, Georgia**

THE BLACK AMERICAN HANDBOOK
FOR SURVIVAL *THROUGH* THE 21ST CENTURY

VOL. I
The Forgotten Truth Behind Racism in America

THE HIDDEN ANCESTRAL IDENTITY
OF THE BLACK AMERICAN
"WHY IT'S A MATTER OF COLOR"

This is a "Must Have" Book For Every "Black American Family"

The Black American Handbook For Survival Through the 21st Century – Volume I

Rev. RaDine Amen-ra

$17.95
(suggested retail price) in U.S.

The logo, as a whole, represents the new symbol of the Legacy of the Ancestral Hentage of Today's Black Amencan People.

The Black American Handbook For Survival Through the 21- Century -Volume I -1-ed.
Rev. Amen-ra, RaDine, 1957
[Book 1 of a Series]

Copyright © 2001 Quantum Leap S.L.C. Publications

Published in Washita by Quantum Leap S.LC. Publications.
All rights reserved. No part of **this** book may be reproduced, utilized or transmitted in any form or by any means, electronic or mechanical, including photocopying, recording - by any information storage and retrieval system without the written permission of the Publisher

Cataloging-in-Publication Data
Rev. Amen-ra, RaDine, 1957
The Black American Handbook For Survival Through the 21a Century -Volume I -1"ed.
p. cm.
Includes Index

ISBN 0-9705455-0-9   ISSN 1531-6688

1. America-Discovery and Exploration   2. Blacks-America-History
3. Indians-Culture.   4. Black American - Geneology

Cover, book & Text design: Steven P Young
"(Ankh & Feather) Hidden Heritage 'Logo Design: Eleye' Eife, © 1999,2000
Authors Photograph (back page) by- John Ziegler
Edited by: Steven P. Young

Printed and bound byFidlar Doubleday
Second Edition:May 2001

The Black American Handbook for Survival Through the 210 Century - Vol. I
Also available on Audio Cassette, Video Cassette and CD-ROM

For more information or to order copies of this book, contact:
Quantum Leap Spiritual Life Center Publications
2740 Greenbriar Parkway, Suite 201
Atlanta, Georgia 30331
1-877-571-9788
Visit our web site at: www.BlackAmmcanHandbook.com

Distributors may also contact: distnbution@BlackAmencanHandBook.com

In loving memory of

The Ancestors

Thomas McCain, Jr. and Viola Baylor McCain

Gone but not Forgotten

Dedication

This book is dedicated to all Black American people, especially The young adults and their children.

To my son Lazar, Victoria, Brianna, Noel, Jackie, Chaz, Alex, Tracey, Devon, Kwame, Javaughn, Alton, Taiomari, Jahnelle, Mrs. Rivers and Grand daddy McCain - there are so many spirits that I can only name a few.

May the Spirit of God fill your hearts and minds with the food of truth, so that ignorance may never be your blindness.

Acknowledgments

I would like to thank all of the wonderful people who have listened and worked with me over the years to unravel this matrix of distortion surrounding my people: Dr. White, Carol Polk, Alisa Dawson, DeAngelo Brown, Antonio Green, Judith Kebe, Karen Stewart, Cliff Stanton, Steven Young, Mother V. Raye, and all of the people who have supported the Quantum Leap Spiritual Life Center over the years... without their support, encouragement and love I would not have maintained the courage to conquer all the obstacles.

In Loving memory of Dr. White.
May these words release his spirit to soar as an eagle,
in triumph.

Author's Note

True Freedom and Harmony among all races of people can only be attained from truth with all races taking responsibility for their actions and effects.

The Black American Handbook Vol.1 is the first of a series of books. This book is only intended to give a balanced overview of the true dynamics that is the core foundation of the United States and its relation to the destiny of Indigenous/Aboriginal American People called Black Americans today.

This book is written in a format that will give the reader a lot of **pertinent facts** quickly. The information contained in these pages will allow Black Americans to identify distorted information. and understand why this distortion exists. It is important for the survival of the Black American people, the who, what, when, where and why must be identified; and which methods are being used to create the deep seated sense of powerlessness we are experiencing as a collective today.

First, understanding who you are must be addressed in order to make the necessary changes toward the survival of the Black American people and their future generations in the rapidly changing landscape within the United States and throughout the world....

Understanding of the whole story gives all the Black American people now living in America a real opportunity to STOP THE DESTRUCTION, ATONE, HEAL FROM THE HOLOCAUST OF THE PAST AND ALLOW THE CREATION of POSITIVE CHANGE FOR THE FUTURE

Table Of Contents

- Introduction
- Heritage
- Preface
- Foreword

I. Profile: The Hidden Racial Identity Of The Original Indigenous North American People Termed Indians ... 1

II. The Hidden Civilization Of Today's Black Americans *(The Vanished Civilization Of The Black American Mound Builders)* ... 32

III. The Hidden Ancestral Identity Of Today's Black Americans ... 56

IV. It Started With Columbus ... 70

V. Understanding Slavery – The Creation Of the "Negro" ... 80

VI. The United States vs. Black America ... 106

VII. Spiritual Understanding Of The Black American Holocaust ... 124

VIII. Conclusion ... 128

IX. Solution ... 134
- Action Plan ... 140
- The Geneva Project ... 141

X. Sacred Journeys ... 144

XI. Appendix: Find your Tribal Nation - List Of Black American Family Names *(English Sir Names)* with Tribal Affiliations ... 145

- Bibliography ... 165
- Index: *Detail of Contents (Question Index)* ... 168

Introduction

In 1984, I had a near death experience that changed my life. During the experience, I asked God, "Why is the experience of being a Black female in America so painful and demoralizing? If I am born a child of God, where is God's love for me and my people? Why was I born to live in a place where I don't belong, where I am unwanted, invisible, and victimized?" I asked God, "Why does being born with beautiful brown skin and soft, fine, curly hair taint me to be treated as an inferior human being?"

I wanted to know who I was. Where did I belong on this earth? Where is the place where I am accepted, respected, protected and cherished, as a valuable part of humanity? Why was I born as a curse to life, and the grace from God to me is death, *not balance harmony and life?*

...Since that time, the Spirit of God has shown me love, given me tremendous insight and exposure to understanding life. In 1986, the Spirit of God led me, first to Egypt. There, I was given the first gift - acknowledgment from the Egyptian people of today, of my Nubian Egyptian Ancestry. I was received with respect and admiration. In Egypt, I noticed the similarities between the Ancient Egyptian symbolism and that of the American Indian. While touring at the mouth of the Crocodile, I asked the Spirit of God, "What happened to my Egyptian Ancestors and where are we today? A beautiful breeze came and, a voice whispered in my ear, Your people are the Egyptians and you live in Egypt. Egypt/Nubia is called America, today. The land of America is where you belong."

introduction

After that revelation, I no longer had the desire to go to Africa. I was secure in knowing that I did not belong in Africa. My heritage may have extended into North Africa but my home, given to me by God, is America.

The *new* question is:

"WHAT HAPPENED TO MY ANCESTORS IN OUR HOMELAND THAT CREATED AN ENVIRONMENT THAT PERPETUATES SPIRITUAL DEMORALIZATION, EMOTIONAL DEPRIVATION, MENTAL- PHYSICAL SELF HATE, and IGNORANCE OF THYSELF (PLANTARY HERITAGE) AS THE CONDITION OF LIFE Black Americans struggle to survive through today?"

I wrote this book with joy and sadness; the joy being that if young adults and children are given some food for their spirit, they can start to counteract the negative cycle of devastation that is looming off the shores in our current future. Maybe, the epitaph that has been written about our extinction as a race of people will not come to pass. Without this vision of hope, I could not write the life-changing information I share with all my people now. The time has come for all Black Americans to look seriously at the condition of life that they are living and why they are living it; to start to investigate what is the truth behind all of the myths and all of the lies.

Heritage

The Heritage is the collective fibers created by **women** that bond to make the fabric of a race. This fabric that is created by women over the ages SUPPORTS the balance in THE SYMBIOTIC MOVEMENT WITHIN ALL LIFE FORMS. (the blending of spirit and matter, creating the divine unity of the spirit in the body). . Heritage contains the knowledge and understanding, why the gift of life on Earth should be respected and taken seriously. The actions from this knowledge unites, strengthens and maintains our life force connection to Nature... THE JOY OF LIFE ON EARTH...

Heritage in part represents the collective actions from the act of Caring for others and our natural environment These acts of bonding unite the family, community; creates the sense of belonging to the group and connection to the natural environment (land), validates the purpose for human life, and gives understanding about the mistakes of the past. Heritage represents the foundation of the culture, which creates the customs, language, religions, practices, beliefs and the unique characteristics that give identity of the group. A person's heritage is the foundation of knowledge that empowers and gives a person a sense of security about their position in the natural world, This knowledge gives a person / group / race the resiliency or power to recognize and counteract the forces of aggression from invaders towards extinction of the race and destruction of the environment that supports the race. Heritage can stop the forces of aggression that deny the

Heritage

natural flow which can restore balance and harmony to their inherited birthright and continuation of future generations to their God given environment for life support on this planet. Ignorance / distortion of one's awareness of their true heritage guarantees confusion/ insecurity about taking responsibility for the person's natural place of belonging to humanity and the environment. This ignorance or distortion of ancestral heritage knowledge effectively disables a person's, group, or race ability to make effective choices that will defend themselves, and future generations from domestication, self-destruction and death.

Pain and suffering is the signal to us from the Spirit of Life. We are out of harmony and balance. We are not listening/ operating from our hearts/ Natural Law. Our perceptions / attitudes towards our lives are wrong, which has denied our natural freedom of Soul expression through ourselves.

Black Americans for the last 140 years to the present, has assimilated into European domestication and has been systematically disenfranchised and disconnected from the roots (heritage) which builds/ supports the spiritual/ mental stability of the race and future generations, as a result Black American people today seek escape by all means possible from the disillusionment and frustration from the emotional insecurity within. The pain is a warning to pay attention, look beyond the illusion of the physical/mind, and go deeper within, for the solution to the challenge. The solution is inherited in the heart of your essence; trust your natural consciousness- Return to Natural Law... Listen and follow your heart, this is where the wisdom of your ancestral

Through the 21st Century – Vol. I

Heritage

heritage (Ancestral Grandmother) is in your BLOOD. The Solution to all challenges is always with returning to, respecting, and following the wisdom of our heritage.

All Black Americans can attest to the fact that their ancestors' sweat, blood and lives was exploited to build the United States. However, it has long been a hidden and ignored fact that the conceptual foundation and the enormous riches claimed by the United States was stolen from the ancestral civilization and heritage from the Nations of Grandmothers from whence today's Black Americans are descendants of…

> *"True comprehension of the past*
> *lends itself to a better grasp*
> *on the present.*
> *It helps us to understand*
> *who we truly are,*
> *and how we came to be*
> *a subjugated people*
> *within this nation today."*

Rev. Rahlae Amen-Ra

The Black American Handbook for Survival

Preface

Today, most Black American elders will tell you that they are not African. They are Indian, Negro or they have some Indian Blood. Most people form Africa will admit to the fact that Black Americans are not their lost relatives. Why do Black American educators and the elite continue to promote West African ancestry for Black Americans, while ignoring the "INDIAN" identity of the elders as the origin of today's Black Americans ancestry?

The intention of this book is to answer questions with facts about the racial identity of the Original American People labeled Indians, what happened to them? How the relationship/agenda of the Europeans towards the Indians in Early American History is the foundation for institutionalized and systematic racism by the United States today, and, the real purpose for the development of Slavery in this land.

The purpose of this book is to help clarify the conflict and confusion Black Americans have today about their real identity and ancestral source. Over the last 70 years, education in Early American "His – story" has omitted the true racial identity of the Indigenous people called Indians and their perpetual enslavement for control of their heritage homeland. Early American History has been replaced with a ROMANTICIZED EUROPEAN version of SOUTHWESTERN INDIANS AND BLACK SLAVES PRESUMED to be FROM AFRICA - CALLED NEGROES.

Preface

However, this is false. Today's Black Americans' perception of the racial identity of the American Indians and the homeland origins of the American Negro is, to say at the least, an inaccurate one.

Today, most Black Americans can identify one or more of their Indian ancestors, while most cannot trace an African ancestor. The confusion about the validity of their Indian Ancestry is based on <u>the perceived racial images of what an American Indian looks like</u> to how the North American people perceive themselves. The racial deception about the identity of the Original American people is so deeply rooted in the United States' past that the truth is repeatedly ignored in favor of the romanticized ideal that maintains its control, exploitation and genocide of the real descendants of the indigenous American people Today, this deception is perpetuated by Hollywood, educational institutions and the mass media.

The deliberate AMNESIA BY THE UNITED STATES OF THE **FACT** THAT THE **RACIAL IDENTITY** OF THE **ORIGINAL AMERICAN INDIAN IS BROWN/BLACK**; THAT THE BLACK AMERICANS ARE THE TRUE INDIANS/ OWNERS OF THIS LAND AS WELL AS THE A SLAVE OF THIS LAND HAS FAR REACHING EFFECTS. The result of this amnesia and deception has created a CONFUSION OF IDENTITY (IDENTITY CRISIS) WITHIN the CONSCIOUSNESS OF today's BLACK AMERICANS Resulting in a DISTORTED ROMANTICISM of BELONGING to WEST AFRICA.

Preface

In return, the real heritage, culture, and homeland of TODAY'S Black Americans as the original North American people and their matriarchal civilization remains invisible. The omission of racial identity of the North American people as Negro, from Early American history in education has left all people, who have adopted America as their New homeland, with a FALSE history. This omission from Early American history in education and through the deception of the media has robbed generations of Black American people of a rich heritage and proud past. Instead this omission has left today's Black American people with no true sense of self and belonging. The real North American (Indigenous) person has become an invisible stranger in her and his own land and is only left with the FALSE version of identity as the "SLAVE" from Western history and propaganda.

The Africans have a saying, "If you don't know who you are, any history will do." "WELCOME TO AMERICA." This is the land where genocide was and is STILL being committed against nations of indigenous people. The fact that Black American people no longer recognize themselves is the core of their ignorance.

Hopefully, this book will start to clear the confusion with facts about the true identity of today's Black American people and give a strong foundation for understanding the reason behind discrimination, institutionalize racism and the systematic destruction of Black American families and communities.

*"A People who have no history
worth mentioning
are likely to believe
that they have no humanity
worth defending.*

They are forever…

…**LOST!**"

Foreword

The following text, at times, may seem to be grammatically incorrect. However, this flaw in writing is done on purpose. I feel that the English language does not afford itself to emotional wholeness, in word form; at times, this may fragment the natural flow of reading and understanding to many Black Americans. I wrote the text to give a clear and precise picture to the reader. I'd rather be grammatically incorrect than correct and vaguely understood, by my reader. So, for those times, forgive me, but the context of the content must not be misunderstood.

Rev

Profile:

A. The Hidden Racial Identity of the Original Indigenous North American People Called Indians

Through the 21ˢᵗ Century – Vol. I

The Hidden Identity

Q: *How many races are there?*
A: Four: Caucasian, Asian, African and Indian.

Q: *What geographical areas do the races of people live?*
A: Each race (and its mixture) has a section of the world.

Q: *Why do all people have a homeland and birthright given to them by God?*
A: All people are the children of the earth. Our mothers are given a land because we require a home, an unconditional place of belonging, and to have a safe place where the environment supports us as we support the environment, a place to be fruitful and multiply. The heritage and culture developed from the environment is where we share our common inheritance of belonging.

Q: *What race do Black Americans represent?*
A: American Indians - Nations of Mound Builders.

Q: *What section of the world do the Indian race inhabit?*
A: Canada, North America, Central America, South America, Alaska, Australia, Pacific Islands and the Caribbean Islands.

Q: *What does the term INDIAN mean?*
A: The word **INDIAN** is the term given to the **DARK-SKINNED PEOPLE LIVING IN THE CARRIBEAN ISLANDS** at the time of discovery by Columbus. It was a term Europeans applied to all dark-skinned people living in North, Central and South America.

The Black American Handbook for Survival

Q: *How many groups of indigenous people lived in North America before discovery?*
A: Three groups. These groups are:
1. The Anasazi people and their civilization called the North to Southeastern Mound Builders (Nubian or Black)
2. The Southwestern Plains – People from the Bearing Strait (Asian/Black mix population)
3. The Northwestern (Russian and Asian mixed population)

Q: *Which group had the largest territory and population in North America?*
A: The Anasazi people and their civilization called the Nations of North and Southeastern Mound Builders (Nubian or Black)

Q: *Which group are today's Black Americans?*
A: The vanished Anasazi people and their civilization called North to Southeastern Nations of Mound Builders; the Planet Keepers.

Q: *Who are the Mound Builders?*
A: The Mound Builders is the name given to the largest indigenous group of people inhabiting North America, and their advanced matriarchal civilization. This master race of Black American people built over 250 thousand earthen-shaped pyramids over the last 12,000 years on the Eastern portion of North and South America and islands. This vast matriarchal

The Hidden Identity

civilization with 400 to 700 million people mysteriously VANISHED during the 1700's.

Q: **How many years did the Anasazi people with their civilization called Mound Builders live here?**

A: Artifacts found in Southeastern America are older than the artifacts uncovered in Egypt, they date back as far as 7,000 to 12,000 years.

Q: **What is a matriarchal civilization?**

A: A matriarchal civilization is a civilization designed by women, around the principles of collective conscience, equality, and oneness. The uninhibited expression of creativity in Nature thru all living forms.

Q: **What do the people who are called the Anasazi or the Mound Builders of North to Southeastern America look like?**

A: Descriptions of the Anasazi people from the Nations of Mound Builders or Cahochez (termed Cherokee), Chickasaw, Creek, Choctaw, and many others.

Letters & Notes on the North American Indians written in 1841, by author George Catlin.

George Catlin, a noted ethnographer describes American Indians as: *"All primitive tribes known in America are dark, copper-colored with jet-black hair."* (Pg.149) *"Some Amerindians have straight hair while most possessed curls in the extreme and every level of wavy hair in between. Texture of the hair is generally fine, soft as silk or coarse and harsh."*

(Today, we call this type of hair "nappy hair". The coarse hair will stand anything and will grow. The fine hair is delicate and considered hair that will not grow because of breakage.)

Catlin also noted, *"The hair of men falling down to the hams and sometimes to the ground, is divided into plaits or slabs two inches width, and filled with a profusion of glue and earth, which becomes very hard and remains unchanged from year to year.* (Today, this form of hair is called "Locks" or "Dread Locks".) Catlin also commented, *"Women used deer oil in their hair and it was long and flowing in plaits or braids. Men wore their hair shaved with a top lock or totally bald."*

Q: **What kind of hair do the real Indigenous North American people have?**

A: Today, it's called "kinky" or wavy hair – not straight.

The Hidden Identity 6

Through the 21st Century – Vol. I

The Black American Handbook for Survival

The Hidden Racial Identity

" The Blisterd Fox, Ioway Medicine Man"

George Catlin, 1841

Could this be the late Redd Foxs great, great grandfather?
Looks just like Redd Fox, Red Fox /Blistered Fox .

Through the 21st Century – Vol. I

Q: **What about the eyes?**
A: Catlin noted, *"Their eyes are black/brown. Eyes can be hazel blue, green, or gray, with mixed complexions from dark brown to very light, as half-breeds."*

And, in the book "Indian America", by Gurko, *"Some have slanted eyes, more did not, noses are high arched, flared or forehead and nose almost flat."*

Q: **What about skin color?**
A: John Smith, the first English explorer, described the color of the people when he landed on the eastern shore of America, in 1612. Today, this location is called Jamestown, Virginia. He described Powhatan, the Algonquin chief he had encountered to look more *"like a devil than a man, with some two hundred or more men as Black as himself."* (Our National Archives, Erik Bruun & Jay Crosby)

John Smith continued, *"Some being very large (tall & big) as the Susquehannocks, others very little (short & petite) as the Wighcocomocos; but generally tall and straight, of a comely proportion, and of shades of brown when they are of any age, but they are born white."*

In Chickasaw Nation, by Mason comments, *"Their complexions are of dark reddish brown or suntan (copper) brown color."*

The Black American Handbook for Survival

Q: **What is the physical stature of the Mound Builders of North America?**

A: (Chickasaw Nation, by Mason) comments, "Men are tall, erect and moderately robust, their limbs well shaped, so generally to form the perfect human figure." (*For example:* Michael Jordan.)

"Women of the Cherokee are tall 5' 7" & up, slender erect delicate frame features with perfect symmetry. Muskogee women are very dark-skinned, short in stature, and well formed. Chickasaw women are a good size as well as beautiful. Delaware women are big and rounded or full figured..."

Catlin makes note of all kinds of different sized and shaped people who are part of the many thousands of tribes living on the eastern seaboard and mountains. In some tribes, the men are 7 feet tall with a large stature.

The word **"TRIBE"** means a **Family, community** or town within a state of the Nation.

Q: **Are there many SKIN color ranges for Anasazi people called American Indians or Amerindians.**

A: Early Spanish explorers noted American Indians were extremely diverse not just in appearance but also in many aspects... Obviously the Indigenous Anasazi people of North American are a race of dark brown /black or reddish brown colored people who are as diverse in phenotypic (physical) characteristics as any other ethnic group.

Through the 21st Century – Vol. I

The Hidden Identity

Q: Do the Anasazi or American Indians of North & Southeastern Nations of Mound Builders people have straight, black hair and tan or white skin?

A: No. This is a myth, pure and simple; perpetuated today by "Hollywood" and the media, in its many forms.

There are no White Indians.

This is a 1822 lithograph of a group of Northern California Indians. Look at the diversity of features. Today the same people would be regarded as Black Americans.

The Black American Handbook for Survival

Catlin did not comment that *some* tribes were dark reddish brown. He stated that **all** Indigenous American people are Reddish brown/ Black. Simply put, the stereotypical white American Indian does not exist.

The truth is that the original Anasazi people called Indians in America are an extremely diverse race of people consisting of Reddish Brown/ Black people of widely varying types that are the real people of the Americas (North, Central, South and Islands) called Indians.

Q: *Are West Africans and American Indians the same people?*

A: No. Both groups of people are dark-skinned however; the skin tone and hue are different.

The skin tone of Indigenous American people is REDDISH BROWN. The darker skin tone and hue of the West African people is quite different.

This explains why most people can tell the difference from a person of African lineage and a Black American – SIMILAR, but not the same.

The term Africans means dark-skinned people from Africa and the term Indian means dark brown or brownish red skinned people from the Americas.

The Hidden Identity

Q: *Well, if Indians are Brown and Africans are black then, what is the real identity of today's Black Americans and how did Europeans tell the difference?*

A: They didn't. All slaves in America ARE the BROWN/BLACK people from the Nations of ANASAZI Mound Builders called AMERIndian people.

The Black American Handbook for Survival

.(This fellow looks like Malcolm Warner from Malcolm and Eddie T.V. show.

This is a water color by Louis Choris, a artist who visited the Spanish mission called San Francisco with members of a Russian naval expedition in 1822. Look at the features, today these people are called Black Americans.

✵

"Sister continents,

Sister races

but not the same

people or continent!"

✵

Black American People are not Africans. The true identity of Black American's are the vanished North America Anasazi Indians

The Black American Handbook for Survival

The Hidden Racial Identity

Q: **How can a dark-skinned person living in America know his true roots?**

A: By believing the oral story of her/his roots from her/his family elders and grandparents.

Black Americans must stop creating confusion and invalidating their ancestry. It is not important to know every grandparent in your family. It is important to know however, which race group your people belong to. If the only word or ancestry you can trace is Indian, then you are.

Q: **What happened to the Nations of Mound Builders' people to make them VANISH in the 1700's?**

A: They didn't vanish at all. They were just re-classified and chose to become INVISIBLE because of the constant, exploitation, invalidation, disrespect, and stealing by the invading European people of their people, heritage and violation of their human rights/ dignity. (humanity) . Forced to accept a new identity by the invading Europeans who wanted claim to their lands, exploit their heritage and harness the technology of the planet from this master race.

All Negro/Brown people born in America represent the last descendants of the first and oldest race of human beings The Anasazi people labeled Nubians / American Indians - termed **Negroes.** The status of this identity means to be raped, de-humanized, and enslaved/controlled by all means possible. This European status was applied to all Anasazi

/Amerindian people, regardless of the fact that they were born free.

This is the foundation for Racism in United States.

However, the difference between the conquest of other nations of peoples and the American Indians was that the English Europeans wanted to permanently occupy the lands that belong to the master race of humans - Nations of Black American Mound builders people (the Anasazi). The English Europeans wanted to replace the Black American people as the master race of planet keepers and develop future generations with bloodline lineage in the Fertile Crescent calling America their new homeland.

"A New Manifest for (Anglo-Saxon/German=Viking) European Destiny"

The difference here is that this environment of land was not developed for or given to them by the Holy Spirit.

For example, take another look at the story of *Goldilocks and the Three Bears*:

Daddy's porridge was too hot (Africa). *Mommy's porridge was too cold* (Europe); *but Baby Bear's porridge was just right* (America). Goldilocks came and **ate it ALL**

UP!!! Not only did Goldielocks eat it all up, she wanted to take Baby Bear's porridge (birthright) now and in the future! Baby Bear must be disposed of and controlled by **ALL** means possible.

As Negroes, the Sovereign North American Nations of Anasazi Mound Builders' connection to their Sovereignty of their lands, identity, culture, and heritage would VANISH; the remaining generations are positioned as permanently subjugated (controlled) people to be exterminated by all means possible by Europeans in their homeland. Today this is called ethnic cleansing of the land.

Over Generations, the new European term for the identity of the Anasazi people (the planet keepers) called Indians becomes NEGROES. As this new term and status was accepted,. the North American people originally termed Indians lost their connection to their true identity, heritage, and land and as a result would stop protecting and nurturing the fertile crescent or heart of the planet called America.

The Anasazi Nations of Mound Builders' (Black Americans) descendants BECAME identified as NEGROES meaning DISPLACED RACE of people who no longer recognized their connection TO THEIR HOMELAND or planet: A PEOPLE WITH NO SENSE OF IDENTITY AND BELONGING… Using

Through the 21st Century – Vol. I

this term Negro/ Black American as a cloak to the real identity. The Anasazi people and their future generations can be domesticated into systems that promote the ethnic cleansing and exploitation of their heritage/ history/ wealth of the race in their homeland and the planet (Europeans now can control/ exploit the world.).

This is the core foundation behind the development of

European Supremacy

Institutional and Systematic Racism in America!

The Black American Handbook for Survival

"Names are like magic
Markers in the Long
and labyrinthine streams
of racial memory
of mankind is stored.
To rob people or countries
of their names is to
set in motion
a psychic disturbance
that can in turn create
a permanent crisis
of identity.
As if to underline this fact,
the theft of
an important place."

(Fulcrums of Change, Jan Carew)

Q: *What happened when the Indians started to accept the European identity as Negroes in the 1700's?*

A: As the Anasazi people from the Nations of Black American Mound Builders, termed Indians by Europeans, accepted the new European status of Negro as their European identity, the children bred from enslaved Black American men with European women could steal / claim the heritage, identity, and land from the enslaved fathers who originally acquired their inheritance of belonging to the land from the Black American women. This reversal of inheritance allowed the European woman to establish the European bloodline as the NEW descendants of the original master Black American race of the Anasazi people in America called Indians and their matriarchal civilization termed the Mound Builders.

Q: *Are the people called Cherokee or North and Southeastern Indians today the real American Indians?*

A: **No.** The people who are considered today as the Five Civilized Tribes / Cherokee Indians or Native Americans are the descendants from the Spanish occupation in America before the establishment of the United States. These people are called Mestizoes. The Mestizoes are people who are mixed with Black American (Indian), Spanish and European (White) blood. They have chosen to adopt the ancestral way of life, culture, and heritage of the original Anasazi

(Black American) people but not their fight or plight. They have no ancestral claim to the land or the heritage (that's why they look like Spanish / Mexicans).

Q: **What does the term "NATIVE AMERICAN" mean?**
A: In the constitution of the UNITED STATES, a Native American is:

1) All persons born within the **jurisdiction of the United States** are considered natives.

2) Natives will be classed into those born before the declaration of our independence and those born since.

3) **All persons, without regard to the place of birth**, who were born before the declaration of independence, who were in the country at the time it was made, and who yield a deliberate assent to it, either express or implied as remaining in the country, are considered as natives.

NATIVES WHO ARE NOT CITIZENS ARE INDIANS AND NEGROES.
Translation: (In other words)
Anybody who was on Anasazi soil called America –that is declared under control by European colonist at the time of the Uniting of the Colonel Coloneys Corporations Declaration of Independence from their European homelands—Creating the United Corprate States.,also included are persons born after the declaration in the United States.are the Native Americans of the United States.(this

Through the 21st Century – Vol. I

The Hidden Identity

maeans everybody or anybody that is not a
Negro=Brown= Indian= Anasazi
Excluded are the orginal people- They are not considered a part of the United States-so they are not classified as Native Americans of the United States
Black Americans are the Natives of America not the United States.
Black Americans are the Indigenous Americans

Q: *Who are classified as Native Americans today?*

A: Anyone with European blood or 3/4 European and 1/4 Indigenous (Black American) Blood can live on reservations: Southwestern and Northwestern Indians.

Q: What tribes make up **the Nations of North & Southeastern Mound Builders?**

A: Cherokee, Chickasaw, Muskogees (Creeks), Choctaw, Black Foot, Osage, Algonquin, Delawares, Tuskarora, Riccaree, Mandan, Washitaw, Tunica, Eastern Sioux (Dah-ca-ta), Shawanos, Yamasse, Pawnee, Assininbons, Minatarees, Crows, Comanche, Oneidas, Senecas, Piankeswhaws, Quapaws, Chippeway, Illinois, Sac and Foxes, Ioway, Cheyenne, Apache, Omahas, Ottos Caddo, Konzas, Potawatomies, Pequots, Miamis, Koiwas, Kaskaskias, Mohawks, Mohegans,

…and thousands more.

The Black American Handbook for Survival

Q: **Why Aren't Black Americans considered Native Americans?**
A: Because you are Indian = Negro. You are considered Indigenous Americans meaning, the original people of the land called America. Today's Native Americans are descendants of European female settlers who had children by enslaved Black American men. They are the foundation for the European bloodline (heritage) connection to the Anasazi land in-heritance called America. This connection to Black American blood gives them partial birthright to the homeland of the Black American / Anasazi Mound Builders people. They are the first European Americans by blood mixing.or miscegenation or ethnic mutation. That is why they are called Native Americans of the United States.

However, the Bloodline inheritance to the homeland only came from the Black American Mound Builders' women, not the men. To claim/ steal the birthright to the land, from the Black American future generations; the Europeans switched the lineage inheritance thru Christianity and their law to the male. This is how the Black American Mound Builders' men/boys were used to steal the land inheritance from their families or tribes to their future generations. This is how the United States stole America.

Q: **Why can most Black Americans today identify with an ancestral Indian grandparent?**

The Hidden Identity

A: Because all Indigenous people from the AMERICAS called Indians are CONSIDERED BLACK / NEGROES.

Q: *Why are my ancestors Indian and I am not?*

A: Whether a person identifies themselves a\s having Black Blood or Indian Blood, you are an American Indian, a descendant of the greatest civilization on Earth. Over the generations of European occupation, the European collective has distorted the racial identity and has constantly invalidated the Black American Ancestral Legacy by renaming our people. The first term for "OUR" Anasazi Ancestors was Indian, the second was Negro. During the 1800's, all Indigenous (Indian) people were under seizure by the invasion of European people coming to claim their land, heritage and to exterminate the Indigenous people, by any means possible.

Millions of our people were dying from disease(germ warfare) or being killed from religious persecutions, LAND and cannibalism. The children were being kidnapped, and young adults were being exported to other islands or other Colonial colonies in America for slavery..

Europeans had no respect for "OUR ANCESTORS' as human beings and were determined to reduce the FUTURE GENERATIONS to homeless remnant savages.*(Example: the humans in the planet of the apes- This movie is a subliminal message of fear to European*

The Black American Handbook for Survival

America of what will happen if Black Americans regain control) To keep your Indigenous Ancestral identity meant to live a life of constant fighting for life. "OUR" Indigenous ANCESTRAL families adopted European names as a way of saving the children who were constantly being STOLEN, raped, and killed by the European people who were coming over to this land in droves to steal everything and anything, and enslaving everyone.

All Indigenous people, labeled American Indian, are Black. This is why there will always be racism in America.

There are only two colors in America: Black represents the Anasazi people, master race of planet keepers; White represents the race that wants to take their place.

Q: *Why didn't my grandparents tell me the whole story?*

A: Mainly because they don't know and the story is filled with memories of living with poverty, pain, demoralization, and fear. This was a result from the constant oppression and destruction from the thousands of immigrating European people who was coming to exploit their homeland. "OUR" INDIAN / NEGRO ANCESTORS, as they were classified, had to learn how to become invisible to their Ancestral identity, rape of their heritage and submit to the status of Slave, in their homeland in order to survive, in the only land they knew.

Yesterday is like today, so many families are constantly being broken up by European intervention. Not too long ago, most Negro children were taken from home by the time they were 7 to 13 years old. Oral history was given while they were young so they would not forget who they were. Over the generations, many elders only remembered that they had "Indian Blood."

Q: **Why do Black American people today dismiss their Indian Ancestral identity?**

A: Today, Black Americans recognize the racial identity and image of their Indian Ancestry as being White instead of recognizing the truth from their elders as being Black.

Today, most Black Americans feel because of the color of their skin and the texture of their hair that they are mixed with African blood. They are not full-blooded indigenous North American people or full-blooded African descendants. They have muted heritage and belong nowhere. This is a European Distortion of the truth. If you are not a person of color, then you are not a true (real) Indigenous American called Indian. Remember, there are no EUROPEAN Indians!

Q: **Why do all Black Americans belong in America?**

A: Today's Black Americans are the real and last of the descendants of the indigenous Anasazi people of the North, Central and South American Nations of Mound

The Black American Handbook for Survival

Builders - termed Indians. **This land is the only land "OUR" Ancestors ever knew.**

That is why it is the homeland for today's Black Americans and the birthright given to them by "The Holy Spirit,"

...STOLEN FROM THEIR ANCESTORS
By
THE UNITED STATES.

The Hidden Identity

William Katz, author of the book Black Indians comments on racial distortion, (page 17):

"*Distorting racial history, as teachers know, injures Dark Children. They live with muted heritage. Despite Black Indians' contributions to their land, neither Negro, nor Indian children, nor the current adult population have awareness of this Legacy.*"

"*LIKE WHITES, Native Americans learned in school that Africans were contented slaves and had no fighting traditions; certainly none that allied them with the Indians. For their part, Afro-Americans are aware of Indians in their family tree but probably assume that like the whites (a further distortion) lurking there, they are mere intruders. Such inaccurate beliefs hide a heritage worth exploring further; dividing people today that could truly benefit from unity.*"

However, this book also maintains the distortion of racial identity. The racial identity of the Indian remains invisible. This omission of racial identity allows the reader to believe the Indians and the Africans were two different races of people distinguished by skin color, and who, by chance, mixed with each other. Of course, the African blood "washed out" the Indian Blood. That's why you have Black Indians when, in fact, they were the same. They were Black American people termed Indians from the Nations of North American Mound Builders, fighting for their freedom to live and not be enslaved.

Even William Katz does not want to tell *that* part of the truth!

The Black American Handbook for Survival

Could this be Little Richards Great, Great Grandfather????

Looks like Little Richard.

The Prophet

The Prophet promised the people they would be immune to the white man's tricks, if they would only return to the old ways.

Picture: George Catlin, North American Indians

Through the 21st Century – Vol. I

(Excerpt from page 149 of
George Catlin's book, written in 1841
"Letter and Notes on the North American Indians")

"All other primitive tribes known in America are dark, copper-colored, with jet black hair. Pardon me, if I lead him through a maze of novelty and mysteries of a strange yet kind and hospitable people, whose fate, like that of all their race, is sealed; whose doom is fixed, to live just long enough to be imperfectly known and then, to fall before the disease or sword of civilizing devastation."

The Black American Handbook for Survival

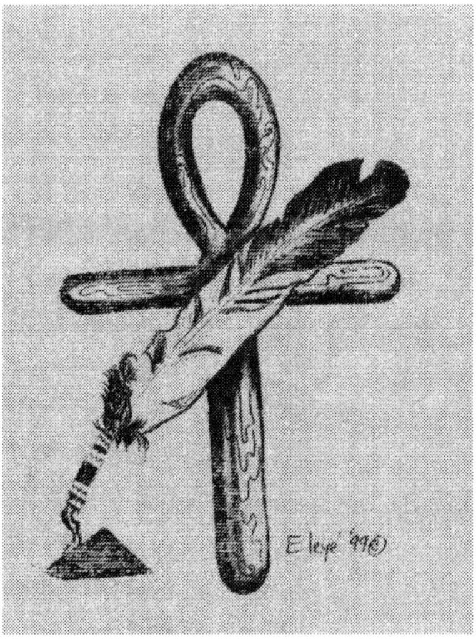
E leye' 99©

Profile:

B. The Hidden Ancestral Civilizations and Heritage of Today's Black Americans

(The Vanished Civilization of the Black American Mound Builders)

The Hidden Civilization

Monument of a vanished people, a huge pyramid-shaped earthen mound built by Anasazi Mound Builders, more than seven (7) centuries ago. Moundville Alabama

(Picture: Time Life Books)

Through the 21st Century – Vol. I

Q: *What was "OUR ANCESTRAL" name?*
A: The Anasazi – meaning Ancient Ones/Planet Keepers

Q: *What does Choctaw mean?*
A: Choctaw means We the People.

Q: *Where did our ancestors come from.?*
A: Originally the continents were one. Africa was a part of the North and South American continent. The North American crescent extended thru North Africa, Ethiopia, into Australia. This is the original Fertile Crescent of humanity. All humanity started in this region and spread from there. Our Ancestors are the remnants of the original human people, and their civilization that created the people of hue (color) today. Our ancestors are the original (the *first*) race of humanity. We were here since the beginning of time. Our Ancestors called themselves the Ancient Ones- the Planet Keepers. This is the reason why the artifacts found in North America pre-date Egypt. Europeans stories from the original meeting with our Ancestors tell the story of how the land was one, and of the event of the Great Flood.

In the Bible, North America is a part of Eden, and our ancestors are the direct descendants of Eve, the Lost Tribes of Israel.

Factoid... The word *Israel* or *Is-real* means (the heart).
In translation, the Lost Tribes of Israel means the lost bloodlines FROM THE HEART OF EVE...

The Black American Handbook for Survival

The Hidden Civilization

Q: *Who are the people from the Bearing Straits?*

A: The Southwestern and Northwestern people migrated from Asia / Russia into the Fertile Crescent called North America from the Bering Straits. These people were migratory people. They live in teepee's and followed the route of the Buffalo. They intermingled and traded with the established Black American communities. Black Americans did not come to American from Asia. Black Americans were here when the Asians came. This distortion has been promoted by the United States so Black American people would not recognize themselves and only see themselves as displaced people.

Q: *What is the name of the North American continent?*

A: To the Ancient Ones the land that is called North America is part of a large Island.

It was called Turtle Island.

Q: *What kind of civilization existed in America?*

A: The oldest, largest female society. The first original form of society in the world. This Matriarchal society represents the human commitment to "fertility" and Nature.

Q: *What kind of society did we have?*

A: Matriarchal, meaning the value system was expressing the feminine principles of nurturing , maintaining harmony , balance .and respect for life . The society was based on equality .and Respect of the difference between man and women. Women were the leaders in most communities.

The bloodline inheritance of belonging to the family and land inheritance came from the woman - <u>not</u> <u>the</u> <u>man</u>. (All children carried their mother's identity).

Q: **What is a Matriarchal society?**
A: Our ancestral society was built around the Mother, but not around one individual woman. All males were regarded as suns of the mother, all females as daughters, and our family included all of nature. Our ancestral society recognized the woman's power as the governing force. This force kept the individual ego aware of its connection to the group and it's responsibility as a member, rather than as an individual in isolation. (Selfish) Our Ancestors understood the purpose of human life on this planet (as planet keepers). They lived harmoniously as they took part individually and collectively in the evolution of the planet.

Q: **What is a "matriarchal consciousness" or "principles of the feminine?"**
A: It is the joy of living. To protect / support the "Power of Creation" in life and nature. That is why our ancestors were called the Planet Keepers.

Q: *What is the meaning of the word America?*
A: The name America or Amerriqui is a Spanish translation of a feminine Mayan term that means *"A Land of Perpetual Life"* or "The Land of the Wind". Sometimes the suffixes "que" and "ikons" mean not only wind or air, but also a Spirit that breathes life itself.

The Land called America is:

"THE LAND THAT BREATHES LIFE!"

or

"The Womb of Life"

Q: *What was the name of our Nation/Empire?*
A: The name of the empire is, by Spanish translation: Cahochez. English translation: (Cherokee) Choctaw.

Q: *What kind of government did we have?*
A: We lived by a Democracy. Our Democracy was fully established for 3,000 years before the arrival of the first European on American shores. It consisted of two parts: the north and southeastern territories

Q: *What is the name of our government?*
A: Ho-Di-No-Sau-Nee, renamed Iroquois Confederacy.

Q: *How big was the original Mound Builders civilization of Black American people?*
A: Our civilization was as far north as Canada; as far south as South America, including Central America and the Caribbean Islands; as Far East as the Mississippi, through Wisconsin, and west into Arkansas.

Q: *Today what States are divided into this land?*
A: Alabama, Arkansas, Colorado, Connecticut,
Delaware, Florida, Georgia, Idaho, Illinois, Indiana, Iowa, Kansas, Kentucky, Louisiana, Maine, Maryland, Massachusetts, Michigan, Mississippi, New Hampshire, New Jersey,
New York, North and South Carolina, Ohio, Oklahoma, Pennsylvania, Rhode Island, Tennessee, Texas, Vermont, Virginia, West Virginia, Wisconsin.

The Hidden Civilization

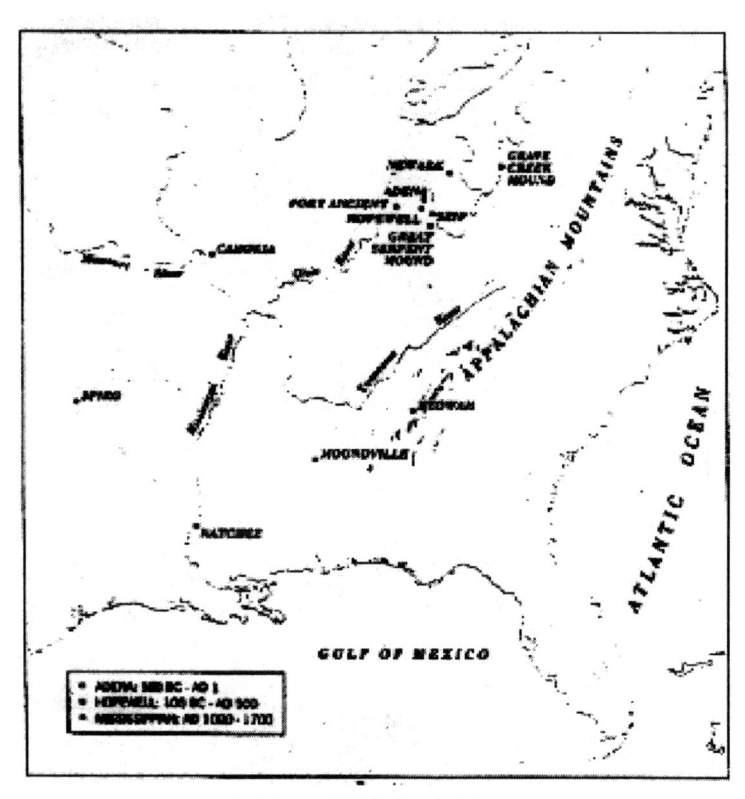

*Adena : 500 B.C – A.D 1
*Hopewell: 100 B.C –A.D 500
*MISSISSIPPIAN: A.D 1000 – 1700 A.D

The map above show how extensive the Mound builders civilization was in North America, The mound builder culture is split up into different time periods. The Mississippian was the most extensive civilization, reaching from the Mississippi valley southeast to Florida, north to Wisconsin and west into Arkansas. However, this thriving civilization with millions of people vanished during the 1700's around the same time all Indians were classified as Negro's.

Through the 21st Century – Vol. I

Reconstruction of a skeleton of an Indian man from Ohio. Observe that many Black American and Caribbean people have this body type today.

Hairdo of the Hopewell Indians of Ohio. A-D and F are bustles, Indian forerunners of a cul-de-Paris, made from turkey tail feathers. Observe the features.

Q: **How many people lived during the Black American Mound builder civilization?**

A: I estimate from my researched calculations, 700 million or at least as many people who currently occupy this land today. The only difference is 95% of the population was Black American or INDIAN. Today we are reduced to 23%, and shrinking.

At the State of the Union Address for the year 2000, President Clinton stated, "It is estimated that there will be no more color in America, in 50 years; thanks to genetic research." He received a standing ovation!! What <u>exactly</u> is he saying?

Q: **How many communities or tribes were here at the time of Discovery?**

A: Thousands or just as many as we have in the United States, today. Most of the town and city names in the United States are names of the actual villages where Black American people lived and flourished for thousands of years. Example: Chesapeake, Illinois, Otto, Pontiac, Wichita, Indian Springs, Tiger, to name a few.

The white-invading settlers squatted on the Black American lands and slowly captured their villages but, never changed the village names.

I recommend finding the origins of the name of your town or city as a research project for young Black Americans. You

Through the 21st Century – Vol. I

will be pleasantly surprised at what they will find, in the treasures of the hidden history.

Q: ***What was our Ancestral form of transportation.?***

A: Our ancestors travel by boat through the interlocking waterways of the North , Central South American continents. All trade was done by boat and interlinking trails.

Q: ***How large was Our Ancestral trade network?***

A: The trade network or economy was based on the development of production from living things. Today this is called commodities. (i.e. beans sugar, tomatoes, silver, and gold, ect.) Our commodities market trade network of our Ancestral (New World) civilization was richer, stronger, and more developed than the old world at that time..Our trade network was very extensive. It expanded from the Northeastern seaboard west through the Rockies into Central and South America. We imported metals as far south as Brazil. *"The Spaniards have never before beheld markets as big as the trading enterprises in our Ancestral capitol, in Central America."* According to Bernal Diaz..

The Hidden Civilization

Q: *What was the character of the Indigenous American Man?*

A: "There are certain qualities of his mind which shine forth in all the luster of natural perception - his simple integrity, his generosity, his unbounded hospitality, his love of truth, and above all, his unshaken fidelity - a sentiment inborn, and standing out so conspicuously in his character, that it has not untruthfully become its characteristic."
(The Savage of America - quote from Lewis Morgan: The League of the Iroquois, 1851)

Q: *What was the character of the indigenous Black American woman?*

A: "In this case, their wives merit their esteem and most gentile treatment, they being industrious, frugal, careful, loving, and affectionate." Always beaming with sunshine- whose sympathetic smiles chased fatigue away and changed the night of melancholy into day. They were truly beautiful and best of all, unconsciously so. *(Chickasaw Nation; Mason 1922)*

Women owned the property, transacted business, and carried on their own affairs freely. A woman's ability to give birth stood not as her exclusive form of "fulfillment" but, as a symbol for her other forms of creativity; and her children were heirs to the female line of descent. There were no illegitimate children.

Through the 21st Century – Vol. I

Q: *What about the Moral character of "OUR" Anasazi or Indigenous Black American Ancestors?*

A: In 1775 – Bartram states, in Chickasaw Nation, pp 487-488: "If we consider them with respect to their private character or in a moral view, they must, I think, claim our approbation <u>if we divest ourselves of prejudice and think freely</u>. As moral men and women they certainly stand in no need of European civilization." "They are just honest, liberal, and hospitable to strangers; considerate, loving, affectionate to their wives and relations; fond of their children; industrious, frugal, temperate, and persevering; charitable and forbearing. I have been weeks and months amongst them and in their towns, and never saw an instance of an Indian beating his wife, or even reproving her in anger. In this case, they stand as examples of reproof to the most civilized nations, as not being defective in justice, gratitude, and good understanding; for indeed their wives merit their esteem and the most gentle treatment, they being industrious, frugal, careful, loving, and affectionate."

(Chickasaw Nation: Mason, 1922)

Q: *What kind of religion did "OUR" Ancestors have?*

A: The Indians (the "Ancient Ones"), by no means, were ever idol worshipers. They only worshiped the Great Spirit: the giver and taker away of the breath of life; with the most profound and respectful homage. (Chickasaw Nation: Mason). Our ancestors recognized that we all connected in Spirit to this planet. We depend upon it for our support, and we are responsible to nature for our gift of life.

Q: **Did we have written language?**
A: Yes our written language was through pictures that represent properties of natural Law. Our ancestors always understood the wholeness of message. Our written language consisted of pictorial messages.

Q: **Did we have Libraries?**
A: Yes, Our Ancestors had hundreds of libraries. The libraries were located in our Mounds. The Mounds kept the heritage, history, and genealogies (bloodline) information about the origins of that peculiar clan of people. The Library also contained the " Secret Teachings". These sacred text explained the complete systems that maintain the planet Earth, its relation to the universe, and the human history upon it. Example: After the raping of one of our Ancestor libraries, Napoleon was able to find what is now called Ancient Egypt. When in fact until the 1700's North Africa was still an unheard of place to the European man.

Q: **What was our main technology?**
A: Agriculture, Botany, Environmental Development, and control over the natural elements; (example: the Rain Dance).

"OUR" Anasazi / Black American ANCESTORS understood every living plant and animal that lives on the land and how to work with them in harmony for many purposes.

Through the 21st Century – Vol. I

Q: *What foods did we cultivate?*

A: Tomatoes, all forms of beans, cabbage, corn, tobacco, sugar, maple syrup, chocolate, coffee, squash, cucumbers, all potatoes (white or sweet), bananas, oats, rice, berries, peanuts, pineapple, avocados, lima, kidney, egg plant, kale, collard greens, turnips, onions, peppers, strawberries, cashew nuts, all herbs, and hundreds of other foods; plants unknown in Europe before the discovery of North America. 90% of all food produced in the United States today are the foods cultivated and produced by the people of the Black American Mound Builders civilization... (the slaves of the United States).

Q: *What was the diet of the Anasazi/ Black American civilization of Mound Builders?*

A: Fish, deer, elk, turkey, some game, but mainly vegetables.

Q: *What kind of clothes did we wear?*

A: When the European arrived, the Anasazi /indigenous Amerindian People had already cultivated cotton and 200 other fibers into cloth. Denim (blue jeans) is an indigenous fabric. Deerskin was used to make shoes, coats, and furniture. Gourds made bowls and clay pots were made, also.

Q: *What were the indigenous Black American Mound Builders' favorite activities?*

A: The SAME ONES WE HAVE TODAY! -PLAYING BALL:Games: BASEBALL, BASKETBALL, and SOCCER are OUR ANCESTRAL sports – they are not from the Europeans. Dancing, singing and music was the Anasazi/ Black American people form of prayer. Dancing, singing and music were so highly cultivated that our Ancestors would dance for all occasions or reasons. Pastime activities also included gambling, numbers, the arts, trade and shopping.

Today, singing, music and dancing are still an important part of our culture, as well as creating art, gambling, lotto and shopping.

The Anasazi /Black American people had the most extensive enterprise trade network in the World. - (Just like today: our people still engage in their heritage; the only difference is, we no longer produce what it takes for our growth and generational survival through enterprise).

Q: *Did today's Black American Mound Builders ANCESTORS have big families?*

A: Yes, the average woman had from 10 to 21 healthy living children. Children were revered as gifts from the Great Spirit.

Children represented the continuation of the ancestral bloodline into the future - Life everlasting!!! Children were cherished, loved, and protected.

Q: *How big was the average family?*

A: The Average Ancestral Black American family was an extended family network - meaning the core group would include the elders, the adults, the young adults, and the many children. Since the average woman produced 15-20 healthy living children, there were always more children than anyone else. The average family could have been as large as 200 people. This would explain why whites called them tribes.

Europeans, upon discovery, had never seen so many young people in their lives. A European woman on average is lucky to produce five children.

Q: *What kind of Education did the children receive?*

A: All children could swim across the river alone by the time they were 5 years old. Children were completely disciplined in behavior, respect for culture, and boundaries by the time they were 5 years old. All children could completely sustain themselves without support from family by the time they were 12 years old. What this meant was that they were able to build a home and cultivate their own food and game, as well as complete training for an enterprise in the arts. Black American ancestors were the originators of the Boy and Girl Scouts ..

Q: *Did we live in tepees?*

A: No. We lived in round-earthen well-established log homes with palisades. Many homes had hot water and saunas. These homes conformed to the natural elements in nature. Our towns and cities were connected by interlocking trade routes. For example: Interstate I-75 was a major route of "OUR" Indigenous (Black) American ANCESTORS used to travel form the northern cities to the southern cities..

Most of today's travel routes in the United States are the trail, roads, and commerce routes for trade developed over thousands of years by the people from the Anasazi Nations or Black American Mound Builders' civilization.

Q: *How long was the life span of Black Americans Indigenous ANCESTORS called the Anasazi?*

A: 100 to 150 years. Many Black Americans today have relatives that live well into there 90's and over 100 years.

Q: *Did our ancestors Develop their own medicine?*

A: Our ancestors knew every plant, and when and where it best grows. She knows every track of bird, insect, reptile, and animal. They knew all signs of weather,

Example from Chickasaw Nation pg 204 " The Indian were thoroughly conversant, it would seem with every herb, bush, and tree in the wilderness within which they lived. Many of these were used for medicinal purposes and with astonishing effect according to the persons who lived amongst them. For instance ,Adair says that, although there were many snakes and many of them poisonous, such as the rattle snake, the Indians had no fear of them, because they compounded herbs which rendered the poison entirely innocuous. He says that when bitten by a venomous snake, the Indian would commence chewing certain herbs with which he was provided and swallowing the same, and although he passed through paroxysms and rigors of pain, that without an exception the poison failed to take effect, and the Indian was soon well. **Likewise they had remedies for nearly every complaint which were very efficacious** - Adair comments.

Q: *Did we have the diseases we have today?*
A: No. There was no form of disease until the European invasion of America. Many Black American people can still remember never being sick with colds or disease.

Q: *What diseases did the European Invaders bring?*
A: Cold, flu, measles, tuberculosis, smallpox, chicken pox, venereal disease, lice, just to name a few. Some disease came with the importation of their animals.

Q: *What animals are NOT indigenous to this land?*
A: Sheep, cows. goats, horses, pigs, chickens, wasps and dogs. Our dog is the fox and coyote

Q: *What foods did the Europeans bring?*
A: Milk, cheeses, bread, wine, whiskey, pasta and sauces.

Q: **What happened to our civilization economy and powerful trade networks.?**
A: All European countries including the Christian church sanctioned the sending of thousands of trading expeditions to our shores to steal the riches, control and enslave the people, rape the resources and destroy our Ancestral matriarchal civilization. take their liberty and

The Black American Handbook for Survival

give them death,(represented by the Statue of Liberty) discover an steal the riches including people. This was done thru trading, raiding and burning our government centers, blocking our routes for commerce and interchange, destroying thru burning our commodities production, this is just a few ways that was implemented to stop and control our commerce and interchange between each other. The Anasazi people could no longer travel freely on their extensive interlocking water and land routes with out fear of persecution, kidnapping or death. from this new invading predator on their land- called the White man… The Black American people had to change and confine themselves into isolated / independent communities or settlements instead of maintaining their ancestral interdependent communities in order to survive. From this fragmentation the Black American peoples control over their vast economy and tremendous commodities production was slowly being dismantled. As a result the European invaders was slowly learning and taking control over the tremendous agricultural commodities, and planetary technology including the vast infrastructure develop over centuries by this advanced race of Black American people. Using this as a foundation the Europeans then developed a country who's main objective of their economy is to control and capitalize on the stolen ancestral technology from the Black American peoples fertile crescent.

Q: ***Did our Ancestors realize the agenda of the European people who was invading our shores?***
A: No, by the time our ancestral collective realized the European was waging a race war against them for the

purpose to eliminate, subjugate and steal their lands. It was too late to stop the invasion against them.

Q: *Why don't Black Americans have a united trade network today?*

A: Over the generations of rape and persistent European destruction of the Anasazi/ Black American civilization, Most Black Americans/Anasazi today no longer have or value the knowledge to produce nor produces any form of support for themselves, they have become dependant (civilized, domesticated) people. To keep Black Americans/Anasazi from re- establishing their independence as a people. The European collective must undermine their efforts for developing self-reliance/ trust with their own group. This is accomplished through discrimination. 'The Black American/Anasazi people are given just enough jobs to survive and become complacent but not enough to re-establish their ancestral independent economy, based on the development of their ancestral commodities. If Black Americans were successful at re-developing their ancestral Anasazi heritage and culture, Black Americans would be recognized again as a viable part of humanity. The world would support the Black American people human rights for self-determination in and on their lands. Black American people could re-build and regain control over their lives and future generations.

This is the reason behind systematic Discrimination!!!

The Black American Handbook for Survival

Black Americans are the real American **Indians-** who are the Anasazi people of North, Central and South American Nations of Mound builders, who lived in balanced and harmoniously operated with-in the natural Life systems, with support, respect, honor, trust and care, which creates emotions of compassion for human life and nature.

Called "Love"
As a result makes life,

" A Joy worth Living"

The Hidden Civilization 54

Picture from: **500 Nations**
Author of Diego Riviera's Views of Tenochtitlans Great Market, Central America: "The Spaniards according to Bernal Diaz, 'had never before beheld any market in size, organization and variety of products and goods'".

Through the 21st Century – Vol. I

The Black American Handbook for Survival

Excerpt from **The 17ᵗʰ Century**

Hostages, Slaves, and Allies

"Unlike the Spaniards, the English were seeking neither gold nor slaves; rather they wanted to tame their new and frequently hostile environment. They needed the Indians' knowledge to help them survive and learn how to exploit their surroundings for their own advantage. Nevertheless, frequent misunderstandings, and even armed conflicts, arose, often as a result of the colonists' greed, as they sought to take possession of more and more land, to control the Indians who lived on it, and to establish permanent settlements. The Indians sometimes realized that, despite treaties and other agreements, the settlers were defrauding them in an attempt to turn them into subject peoples."

THE

HIDDEN ANCESTRAL IDENTITY

OF Today's Black Americans

The Black American Handbook for Survival

Queen Neferetiti appears quite Caucasoid in this famous portrait. Today it is known that her blood relatives had kinky hair and Indian/Negro features. Neferetiti's family like any of today's Black families appears to have included a wide range of physical types

In this stone carved portrait of Neferetiti in Egypt it is clear she has Negroid features. Today many Black American women have these features. It is clear to anyone looking she is not of Caucasoid decent.

Q: *Who are the indigenous Black Americans in the Old Testament in the Bible?*
A: The Children of Messina/Moses, "The Hebrews".

Q: *Are Indigenous Black American or Anasazi Nations of Mound Builders the people who were given, as promised by God, a new Homeland?*
A: Yes. The Anasazi people or the Black American Mound Builders called Indians are the Children of Israel (the word "Israel" means heart), mentioned in the second book of the Pentateuch and the second book of the Bible, Exodus, who were instructed by the Holy Spirit to leave North Africa (Egypt) for a new homeland before the great flood which separated the continents.

(At this time I must make note, however that Egyptian artifacts in North and South America pre-date Egypt by thousands of years, I am inclined to believe that the exodus was <u>reversed</u> from North America to Egypt. I am also inclined to believe that there was an expulsion of the people who chose to be irresponsible to the planet- by consuming for selfish pleasure the earth's planetary resources. These people were forced by the larger group of Black American ancestors to find a new location in the Fertile Crescent. These people are the people who built Egypt. .)

    The remaining Black American (Anasazi) ancestors maintained the fertile crescent (North - South America and Islands) as homeland and continued to live in true spiritual and religious consciousness. However, in the European King James prescribed translation of the Hebrew old testament in the Bible, the Exodus is reversed and some text omitted; i.e. racial identity of Hebrews is Nubian= Negro.)

In the European King James version of the Bible the children of Israel or Black American ancestors were given the fertile homeland as deliverance of true spiritual and religious consciousness. The Ancestors of today's Black American ancestors called Negro's were delivered from the obscurity, darkness, and ignorance of the growing NEGATIVE wave of Male supremacy/ Patriarchal consciousness or the "mind of the flesh" (the Ego). This doctrine of exploiting women and consuming nature was changing the once Northeastern forest area of Kemit called North Africa today into a barren desert called Egypt.

In the new land, the Children of Israel/ Anasazi people or the Black American Mound Builders RESPECTED LIFE IN <u>ALL</u> FORMS, followed the laws that governed nature, and supported life on this planet. (Great Spirit). The people built huge tabernacles towards the sky called Mounds. Our Black American Ancestors understood the destruction that would come to them if they did not honor their environment and support their responsibility to & for it.

The Black American Mound Builders NEVER worshiped or placed a higher value over any life forms created by the Holy Spirit including man.

They Never saw MAN AS equal to or lawgiver for spirit. Natural law was the governing force of the planet and all its millions of creations...All life systems are valuable.

Through the 21st Century – Vol. I

Q: *What happened to the people who lived in North Africa who chose to live self centered and consume nature.*

A. As the resources dwindled a power struggle insured between the Kemmit/ Egyptian man and women for control of the planetary resources. Ramsey an Egyptian ruler decided to make himself a God and place all life forms under his domain for control and consumption. Before Ramsey the Egyptian people worshipped the different forms of natural expression with deities. Ramsey declared that all forms of natural expression was now him and him alone. He became the maker, the ruler, and the keeper of human life (i.e.; the father, the son and the Holy Ghost)_ and all living forms on earth. He is regarded as the father of Patriarchal Thought. **Mans worship of Man and HIS false idols (MONEY, Gold, Silver, etc.)**

Q: *What happened after Ramsey declared himself a God over Egypt or Kemmit.*

A: Under Ramsey's rule, the brutal, aggressive changeover from one form of culture to another starts to unfold. The equalitarian society is replaced by a society of dominance and submission. This makes a fertile atmosphere for the development of, corruption and consumption. This sift of thinking consequently destroyed the part of the fertile crescent located in North Africa which created the buried ruins of Egypt we know of today.

Q: *What is a Patriarchal consciousness? The taking away the joy of living on Earth...*

A: A state of separation from the unconsciousness connection to the natural World. The separation of ego empowered by intellect from its connection to spirit and nature. . The spirit of nature becomes invisible and is no longer recognized in the physical world. Operating As an individual in isolation, the world is devoid of feeling, everything exist outside and independent of self. All living forms are to be used as objects, no different than a craftsman uses materials. The living world becomes the prey of mankind. Instead of man being the supporter of life he is now the predator against life. (Note: it is also written that during the Indo- Aryan time period (second and first millennia B.C.) of the astrological age of Aries this form of consciousness was pre-dominant with the ancestors of the European people.

Q: *What is a Patriarchal society?*
A: A society that is governed by the doctrine of male supremacy thru the use of fear, suppression, submission and dominance for the control of fertility and nature. The overriding factor to maintain this society is to remove the female control over birth and the healing power of unity thru female sexuality.

Q: *How did the patriarchal take over the Matriarchal way of living?*
A: All forms of Rape percussion was used and became the main institutionalized form of gaining social control over the young female and woman. and their ability to support nature. Fear of physical torture in the form of Rape keeps all women in a state of fear. Women had no need for male protection before men adopted a consciousness in which it is men themselves whom women have to fear.

Q: *What happened to Kemmit or Egypt after the raping, killing and enslavement of the women by the men?*

A: The North African environment and the remaining women of the Bloodline stopped reproducing and started dying; a female shortage ensued forcing the remaining survivors of the generations of men to search, invade and conquer other areas of land for survival and consumption of the environmental resources that maintain and support life. They were forced to seek out smaller bands of people in Asia Minor to rape, exploit and enslave women to make children, which created the bloodline of the Nations of Arabic People.

Q: *What is the name of the people who are the remaining descendants of the Egyptians of North Africa?*

A: They are called Muirs. /Moors

Q: *Who are the Muirs / Moors?*

A: The original people called Moors are the surviving descendants of the Egyptian people who lived in North Africa, who raided the land of Kush (lower Africa), conquered the Slavic people from eastern Europe migrating to Southern, Western Europe and Asia for the purpose of sexual exploitation and proliferation with women for children.

Over hundreds of years, the blood mixing by North African (Black) men with Slavic (White) women created the 15th century Muirs/ Moors of Spain/Portugal. and Italy. These are the children of mixed blood relations from North African men and Slavic (European) women. Morocco, Arab and many Islamic (Middle East) nations today are of Moorish descent.

The Black American Handbook for Survival

Q: *What does the word "Slave" mean?*

A: The word "slave" is a slang word meaning "Slavic" representing the savage European (white) people who were inferior and controlled by the North Africans.

Ironically, at one time, if a person was white, it represented the same treatment Black Americans receive today. All European people were given the identity as savages, because of their hedonism/ preditoristic living systems. They were considered as inferior humans.. When the Europeans invaded America, they switched their sordid history and forced their inferior hedenonist life systems on the Black American people.

Black American people should NEVER be embarrassed by the term "slave" because it will never represent them. Black Americans can never be of Slavic decent the word "slave" represents. Therefore, Black Americans can NEVER be the DESCENDANTS OF SLAVES.

Q: *Are the Moors and the Black American Mound Builders called Indians the same people?*

A: No. Anasazi/ Black American Ancestors lived on this land for thousands of years. They are not mixed with Slavic blood. The people who are called Moors discovered our Ancestors, in the 1500's. "OUR" Indigenous Black American Ancestors were not responsible for "Slavic" Slavery. However, our very distant remaining Egyptian/Muir cousins living in North Africa were.

Q: *What do Nubia, Atlantis, Egyptians, Hebrews, Omecs, Aztecs, Mayans, Mound Builders, Indians, Negroes, Mulattoes, Colored, Afro-Americans, and Black Americans have in common?*
A: They are all the same race of people with the same identity; reclassified with different names to represent different world times, by European people

Q: **Do the North African Moors have claim to the Ancestral Homeland as the Indigenous/ Anasazi/ Black Americans?**
A: No. The Moors, as MEN, are the People who <u>started</u> the rape of the Anasazi people, their civilization and the land as commerce for European consumption, in America. Their purpose was to start commerce from capturing women and boys, to sell in Spain and Europe as sex toys.

The fervor that was created by the physical beauty and healthiness of the Anasazi-Indian- Negro Bloodline (young male was captured) for procreation and the beauty of the Indigenous Young female children and women for sadistic sexual violation and exploitation started the subsequent invasion by thousands of men from European Nations, called explorers, to conquer America for women, young adults and land. - *Just like today, our Nubian cousins living in the Sudan. Thousands of young women and children are being captured and sold as (concubines); Slavery is one of the oldest forms of ethnic cleansing.*

Q: *How did the European people regain control of their heritage from the Muirs?*

A: Over time the European women discovered that their fertility increased from mating with Nubian/Muir/ Black American men. The Nubian mans sexual energy actually feeds the European woman with life giving energy. . The Muir men thought they were rapping the European women, when in fact the European women was consuming the Nubian man's life force thru sex for procreation of children and for the harvesting of genetic environmental inheritance of strength and fertility in the Nubian bloodlines to be transferred to their children (Boys).. Thus…. Insuring the survival of their race and power for their future generations. Procreation from blood mixing, as a result from the sexual seduction of the European women towards the Nubian man, made the European people stronger. By the time the Muirs realized the seriousness of this sexual mistake called miscegenation. . their was not enough full blooded Muirs to hold the control over the European people and could be easily exterminated…

In Chickasaw Nation, PG 383. De Tocqueville opinion about the fate of the Southern States in this comment he sites the fate of the Moors in Spain.

" The fate of the White population of the Southern States will, perhaps be similar to that of the Moors in Spain. After having occupied the land for centuries, it will perhaps be forced to retire to the country whence its ancestors came, and to abandon to the Negroes the possession of a territory which Providence seems to have more peculiarly for them, since they can subsist and labor in it more easily than the whites."

The Chickasaw Nation 1922 pg 383

"Black Man",
It is time to respect and understand
Who you are!"

The Black American Handbook for Survival

"Black Americans, it is time to understand Who you are!"

The Anasazi = The Ancient Ones

Negro's / Black Americans / Indians / Nubians / Egyptians

Through the 21st Century – Vol. I

It started with

COLUMBUS!

Q: **Who authorized Columbus military voyage?**

A: Queen Isabella and her consort Fernando from Spain in 1492.

Q: **What was the purpose for the expeditions to find new lands of Columbus?**

A: The coastal areas of Africa were becoming sparse of people and the Spaniards had to go further inland to capture people. The people from the coast of Africa were fighting the Spanish invaders. The Spanish predators had to look elsewhere for more fertile or populated areas to exploit and consume people.

Q: **Why did Columbus choose to sail across the sea?**

A: The Muir's/ Moors spoke of legends of the missing tribes of Israel and their perfect civilization with recourse rich lands, that was across the sea.

Q: **What kind of society did the Spanish need to find in order to conquer them?**

A: The Spanish predators needed to find people who were operating as natural humans, in matriarchal societies. They had to be innocent to the ways of mankind.

Q; **Why is it important to the European predators to seek out races of people who are operating in an unconscious state of wholeness with the planet?**

A: People who are operating in natural systems do not look at life in an offensive manner; therefore there is no need to over develop the predator instinct in them. There societies for the most part are open to receive the different, the new, there is trust and sharing for all. Life is respected and shone compassion. Compassion is what life is about, there is no need to fight or consume, defend or live in great fear of other apparently human beings. Military is developed in defense only-- not in offense. Secrecy is not necessary. People who are operating from love have no need to fear

. Q: **What would the Europeans have to do in order to break the protection that the races of the planet had from living in natural Law?**

A: The people had to be seduced into selfishness and concepts of self-importance over other living forms. The ego had to be given a mind set for separation from their heart and spirit. When this starts to happen a split is started between the man, the women and all life forms that support them. The mans ego will be influenced to isolate himself and become a predator to his own life force. Once this is done the man loses all of his holy perfection, balance and protection. The man is now blind to the weapons of the predator. He is now open to be consumed by mankind along with all that has been placed in his grace. The more experienced predator now has the human naked and without his spiritual protection and

The Black American Handbook for Survival

shields. The predator now can tear his heart out, cripple him to his knees, exploit. rape, control his ability to produce, provide and protect his power source within the woman, child. and nature.

Q *Did Columbus discover North America?*

A: No. Columbus discovered an island across the ocean from Spain. Columbus named it Hispaniola. Today it is called Haiti/Dominican Republic. This new area of land was heavily populated **with light- dark brown skinned people (Anasazi /Red/Nubian= Negroes)** who had a higher standard of living than the Spaniards and an advanced matriarchal civilization with enormous agricultural technology and natural resources. Columbus named these DarkREDDISH/ brown -COPPER COLORED (Anasazi /NUBIAN) people Indians

Meaning indigenous=original

Unfortunately, The direction he thought the land of milk and honey was in , today is called India, however this is not the land he actually discovered. Instead, he discovered many islands that had millions of beautiful Nubian (Red/Brown) humans who HAD enormous land resources:

Q: *Why is Columbus given credit for finding the Americas?*

A: Columbus is famous for finding the oldest living human race /society in the world and civilization with enormous

It started with Columbus

resources that could be exploited for an endless supply of Natural commerce for wealth in the European dominions.

Finding the Land of Milk and Honey...

    The Fertile Crescent of Humanity.

        The Ancient Ones.....

            ...coined The New World.

Q: *What was the original color for the European term Red?*

A: Brown was the original color for the term Red until the 1800's. The color we know as red today was not classified as red until the coming to the New World.

Q: *What did this land look like at the time of Spanish Moor discovery?*

A: Every Early account tells of the marvelously beautiful and fertile land, the magnificent forests, the clear and quiet lakes, the vast stretches of flowering woodland crossed by sweet-water brooks. The land was not only beautiful to look at but abundantly filled with game and food of every kind. To the European, this land was Eden.

Q: *What happened after Christopher Columbus discovered the New World?*

A: The land was divided into two territories: Spain had full dominion to exploit Central and North America; Portugal was given dominion to exploit South America..

The Black American Handbook for Survival

Q: **When was the Mainland of North America discovered?**
A: Around 1509-1540. Juan Ponce de Leon 1513, Lucas Vazquez de Ayllion 1526, and Hernando de Soto 1537.

Q: **What was used to create a division in the America's between the Woman and Man?**
A: The introduction of European technology. The physiological technology was Christianity; the physical technology was the gun. Convincing the Black American men they were weaker than the white man because of his development of the gun.
because of the mighty gun. The white man God was more powerful and the owner of the planet. (Even though the Black man won most of the wars against the white invaders)

Note: Today Black American men are considered weaker in the mind to white men, because they still have not been able to master their own ego's. therefore fail to recognize how to stop falling for the weapons of false and physical illusions that has been projected to them.

Q: **What did the Spanish do to implement Patriarchal religion of Christianity into the American people?**
A: The Catholic Christian Church in the Name of Jesus condoned the killing of men, the stealing of children, the rapping and burning of millions of innocent women in there villages, if they did not convert to be willing slaves. *(After they converted however, In the name of Jesus the captured American people were fed to the dogs.)*

In Christianity the power of writing became the right to have power over. Writing, which was used as a sacred expression of spiritual thought, became a deadly tool of the predator, to be used by the ego to dominate people and exploit nature. Just as it used today.

Q: ***What is the difference of Patriarchal religion and Matriarchal religion?***
A: In Patriarchal religion; Life is a veritable crucifixion; in Matriarchal religion life is a gift of joy...

The Patriarchal pathology for religion;

In order to earn the love of the Supreme Man you cannot have compassion, care, concern or respect (love) for anything in life including yourself.... You live to be united with him when you release your gift of life (once fully understood it makes a person wonder is heaven really hell?). The woman who represents the portal for regeneration of human life now is projected as unclean, material, instinctual, evil, sensually, wicked and sexually gross.

The Black American Handbook for Survival

Excerpt from
**The 17th Century Hostages,
Slaves, and Allies**

"By the end of the 16th century, France, Spain, Portugal, and England were attempting to establish colonies in the New World. They made little change in their previous harsh patterns of exploitation and settlement, and the relentless onslaught of European explorers, traders, and armies took its toll on the Indians. They at first welcomed the newcomers but, as before, saw their hospitality repaid with treachery, and watched in horror as their people died from the effects of war, disease, and religious persecution.

The papal bull of 1493 allocated Brazil, alone of the countries in the New World, to Portugal, which consequently confined its activities to exploiting that region. Elsewhere, the wave of conquest spread north from South America and Mexico through what is known today as the Southwestern United States and the eastern seaboard. Although the Indians soon realized the advantages of European trade and technology, they sometimes understood too late that with them came the introduction of European ideas and culture that caused a schism and demoralization among themselves. Some Indians willingly ceded their lands.

Through the 21st Century – Vol. I

It started with Columbus 78

1519

Spanish often amused themselves by encouraging their "pets" to tear unarmed Indians apart and eat them alive.

Reproduced from the collections of the Library of Congress

Reproduced from the collections of the Library of Congress

1568

Some of the wanton cruelty that was inflicted against the Indians. Hernando De Soto's expedition capriciously mutilated and tortured Indians for no apparent reason

The Black American Handbook for Survival

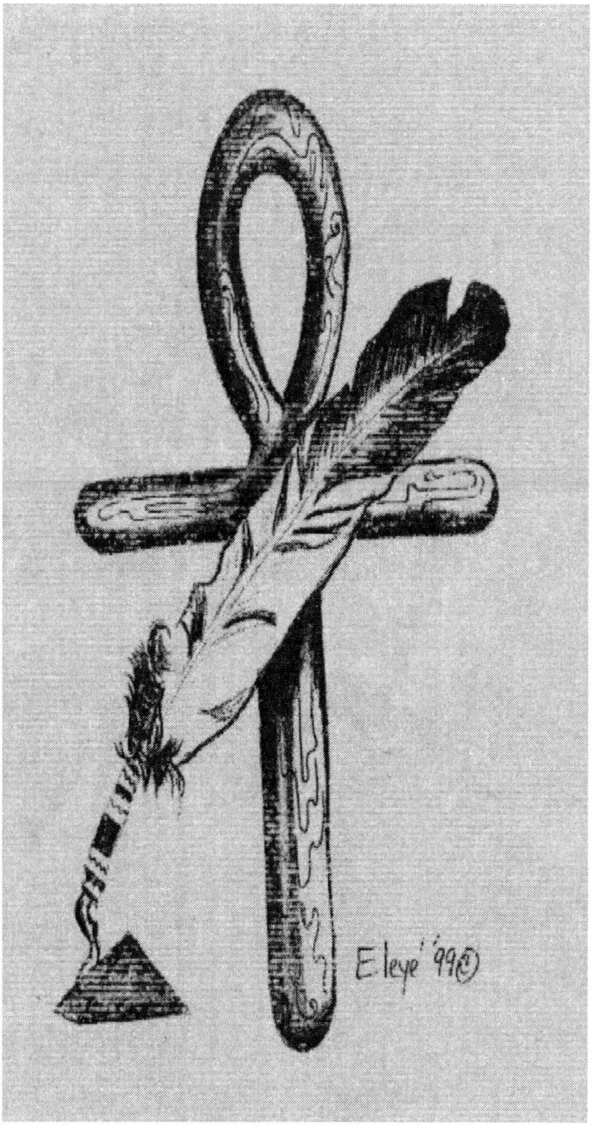
E. Ieye' '99©

UNDERSTANDING SLAVERY

The Black American Handbook for Survival

Today most Black Americans think of Slavery as African people being thrown on a boat and brought thousands of miles without food and fresh water straight to America. However, the reason behind human bondage and perpetual subjugation has never been addressed. All Black American must understand the real agenda behind the institution of slavery in North America by the European colonist under English " Color of their law". Black Americans today must realize the truth about slavery/ racism/ in America as a form of ethnic cleansing and how any distortion of the truth maintains their genocide and physiological (mental) bondage.

Q: *What is the purpose of capturing and using people for mechanical labor?*

A: The purpose of using people as mechanical machines is to extract as much production from them that their life force energy will produce. It is no different than using a battery. A person uses all of the energy that can be produced within the elements of the battery for their own use, with no regard to the regenerative needs of the battery. Once the battery is depleted of its core elements to create energy, it is considered dead and then discarded. The same attitude is applied to people (as slaves). However, why different groups of people chose the use of harnessing human energy by the collection of people has many different reasons - mainly to extract from others what they don't have the ability to do themselves. The people who lived in their regions always knew where and how to collect, extract or produce from their environmental habitats. Example: Indians knew how to grow the foods of this land.

Through the 21st Century – Vol. I

Understanding Slavery 82

Q: *How many races have experienced being robbed or enslaved during their history?*
A: All races have had some group of people choosing to extract and steal from their environment, including their young people, and the riches that God gave them.

For example: *"Raiders of the Lost Ark"*. This movie is about stealing the Ark of the Covenant from North Africa. The reason was to prevent the indigenous people to whom it presently belong to for thousands of years or any other people from ever being able to use its power for aggression / exploitation against the United States. *(However, what protects other races of people and lands from the aggressions/exploitation of the United States?)* This reason justifies the theft. The Ark is now located in Washington, D.C., in the archives of stolen worldly treasures, according to the movie. The raider/ thief is considered a hero, because it is a win –win situation for the United States. This is the ethics of United States.

....NOW, IT IS IN *SAFE* HANDS....

Q: *When did Slavery Start?*
A: The cycle for people of color started in North Africa with the Moors. It started for the Europeans with the Vikings. The European race has always been the exact opposite from the races of color. Races of color are agricultural and Europeans are predators, meaning people who feed on death. (Flesh eaters)

The Black American Handbook for Survival

Q: ***Who would have to be enslaved for the knowledge to produce from the environment in America?***
A: The young adults and children of the Anasazi people. The Europeans did not have the knowledge of the environment in America, neither did the Africans. Africans could not grow produce that was foreign to their habitats. Production from America's natural resources from European or African people would be highly impossible.

Q: ***How long did European Slavery thrive in West Africa?***
A: 1100 - 1400's

Q: ***Where were the West African people transported to?***
A: Spain, Portugal, South America, and Europe.

Q: ***When did Slavery start in North America?***
A: In 1513, with the first Spanish expedition.

Q: ***Were Africans brought over to America, in the 1500's?***
A: No. The first people brought over to this land as slaves were Indian Cubans with the Lucas Vazquez expedition. Once Indians were captured they were referred to as Negroes.

Understanding Slavery 84

World History Atlas depicts the African slave trade to be between the North and South American continents .not between Africa and North America. Does this map represent Slave trade of Africans or Indians? The use of the term Negro as the same as African has distorted the real Holocaust story of what happened to today's Negro American Ancestors who are Indians.

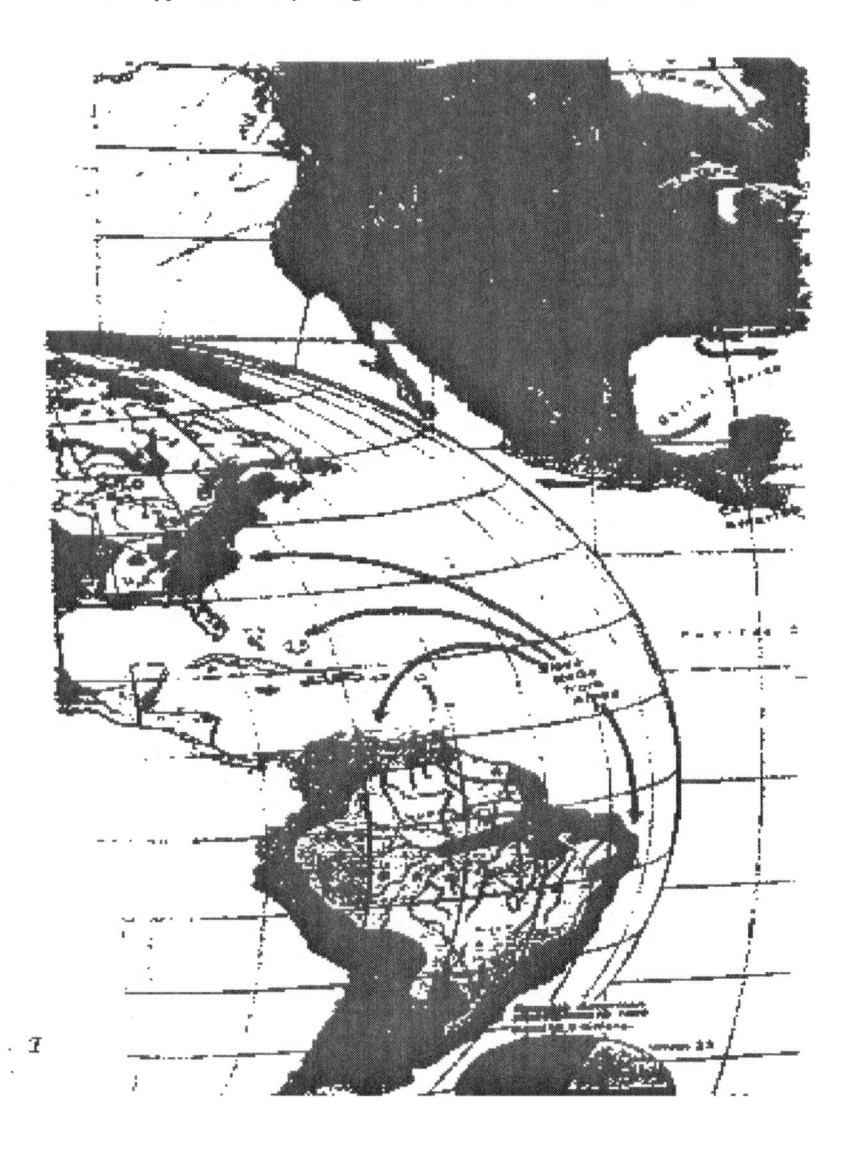

The Black American Handbook for Survival

Q: **What is the percentage of Africans who came as slaves to North America?**

A: Less that 3% of the North American Slaves were acquired from villages within Africa. The majority of slaves came from the stealing Anasazi children from the North and Southeastern Nations of the Mound Builders. The older adults captured were imported to the West Indies. People were also brought to the West Indies from South America, not Africa.

Q: **Why didn't Europeans bring Africans over to North America?**

A: Because the African people were fighting the Europeans, starting in the late 1400's. The West African people understood the European system and could teach the Indians, "OUR ANCESTORS", about their customs and ways. Europeans were afraid that if Indians and Africans mixed, the Africans could tell the Black American Indians how the European system worked to enable the Indians to overpower the Europeans, this might bring the result of the consumption of European Wealth and start the re-enslavement of the European people. In order to control and subjugate the Nations of Black American people, the Europeans knew that they had to keep the them ignorant and innocent to understanding the European agenda of genocide for them.

Q: **Where were the Africans and Indians taken to?**

A: Most of the African slaves were sent to South America. There are treaties forbidding Africans to be enslaved with

Indians on the Indian homeland. Now, when you watch the movie, "Amistad", you will understand why, once the people were able to prove they were African, they were released.

Q: *So where could Africans and Indians mix?*
A: In the Antilles. Today this is called the Caribbean. That is why people from the Caribbean Islands are called WEST-INDIANS, MEANING WEST AFRICANS *MIXED* WITH NORTH, CENTRAL AND SOUTH AMERICAN INDIANS. Even though a very small percentage are mixed with West African blood, they can have a large percentage of South American Indian blood. The people from the Caribbean are actually Black American's long lost ancestors from North and Central America deposited there by the Europeans. The Caribbean dialect is the original dialect of the Black American people.

Q: *What European countries participated in the slave trade of the North and South Anasazi American people- called Indians termed Negro's?*
A: Spain, Portugal, France, England, Italy, Great Britain, Germany, Sweden, Scotland, also sea traders from the Ottoman Empire (Iran, Iraq and Turkey).

Q: *How was the first economic trade started for Europeans in North America?*
A: Hit and run raids on villages to capture women, children and young men for the purpose of human bondage or used as sex toys for EXPORTATION ALL OVER EUROPE, the WEST INDIES, and COASTAL NORTH AFRICA.

The Black American Handbook for Survival

Q: ***Do Black Americans have West African Ancestry?***
A: Not from slavery. Africans are considered free people. Unless you can directly trace it, you don't have it.

Q: ***What was the average life span of a person once captured in the 1500's –1700's?***
A: You worked until you died - 6 weeks, if you were lucky.

Q: ***How did the Europeans conquer "OUR" Indigenous ANCESTORS?***
A: First, the explorers would appear… then, the Christian missionaries… then, the traders and whiskey… then, the settlers, the diseases, and at last, **the army**.

Q: ***How did the Europeans capture large numbers of people?***
A: **First**, by offering whiskey and wine to the men.
Second, convincing the men about their concept of God. The White man's God puts man in charge over women and life. Man is not to be held responsible for their actions. Why? Because someone else has taken the responsibility (Jesus).
Third, by coercing the Indigenous Americans to participate in the European trading matrix of exploiting there human and natural resources.

Excerpts from,
The pages of Letters and Notes
on the North American Indians,
George Catlin, (page 89):

"The Indians of the forest and prairies of North America are a subject of great interest and some importance to the human investigation, whose early history is LOST: whose term of national existence is nearly expired; three fourths of whose country has fallen into the possession of civilized man within a short space of two hundred and fifty years. Twelve million of whose bodies have fattened the soil in the meantime; who have fallen victims to whisky (liquor), the small pox (disease), and the bayonet (guns), leaving at this time but a meager proportion to live a short time longer, in certain apprehension of soon sharing the same fate."

Q: ***What is the Profile of a slave?***
A: Most people were women, young adults and children. The older adults were killed. The people were always walked or shipped to a new location within their region. The young adult women were always sodomized, shipped and sold as sex slaves. The young boys were always beaten, sodomized to be sold as sex toys for men. The men were used in the mines, or to build railroads, and the best looking would be used to sexually gratify and procreate with European women. This is where the stories of the Black American's sex power come. European women wanted to procreate for children so the genetic power in the blood of the race could be harnessed for their future generations.

Q: ***How long did the exportation of "OUR" Indigenous Black American Ancestors exist as slaves?***
A: Exportation stopped to European and North African countries by the late 1700's; however, exportation from the mainland to the Islands and 13 colonies existed until 1870.

The creation of the " American Negro"

Q: **What was different about the English agenda for Slavery?**

A: The European colonist consisting of German, Irish, English, and Jewish people wanted more than to conquer and exploit, they wanted to permanently control and live in the Anasazi people land, replace their heritage with his-story, steal their agricultural technology and the riches from their civilizations. In order to do this the European people would have to disconnect the future generations of Anasazi people from their ancestry, identity, heritage, culture, language, civilization and ultimately the land in order to erase the race of people from the land. Slavery is the first step.

Note: The old worldview was to conquer and steal people and resources from their lands. All people kept their identity; they lost control over their self-determination for their future generations

Q; **How did the European colonist apply their agenda through slavery?**

A: In order to accomplish this, the colonist must steal the children from the Black American woman, especially the male child. They had to stop the transference of information to the Black American children about their identity, heritage, culture, language, place of natural belonging to the land, total understanding of the war

The Black American Handbook for Survival

that is being raged against them, their people and why. The children had to become ignorant to who they are, where they belong, their connection to humanity, and made to accept -because of this, they are inferior humans and must live as subjects to the European people. Black American children were being stolen by the colonist, shipped to different locations to be stripped into this new mental identity. Children who fought were called juvenile delinquents. The young men and women who escaped called (maroons) who tried to start new communities, when found were burned and killed. The Black American people villages were r constantly being raided for their young people by the white settlers looking to steal more land and establish their bloodline for ownership. The Anasazi people and their civilization was being torn apart from its heart (their children).

Q: *How did the acquisition of children for the slave trade in Anasazi people termed - Indians work between colonies?*

A: In order for Europeans to control/claim the land, they would burn down the villages and towns, seize, capture and branded the people of the area. Once branded, the Indigenous (Black American) person would be shipped off of the land, to be processed at another colony that was established on the eastern coast.

That is why the eastern coast of America does not have huge stadiums for the importation of people.

Through the 21st Century – Vol. I

For example: if a 15 year old person was caught in New Jersey, they would be taken to a white settlement, transported to the shore, put on a ship, and sent downstream to South Carolina. It could be done in a couple of weeks (there is no need to feed cloth or give water, you can also pack the people in like sardines without a great loss of life). Once a shore they would be processed as a Negro into the plantation system and sold as property. to other European settlers

Q: *What does "Branding," mean?*
A: Once a person is captured in their village, all the belongings within the village and clothing are taken from the village to the White settlements.. The surviving people are only left with what is needed to cover their private parts. Children are left naked. Then a hot iron with the symbol of the trader/buyer is placed on their flesh in a highly visible place; i.e., face, neck or upper shoulder. Once branded a person was given a new name and recorded under the buyer. (A paper trail was started on the person)

Q: *What has to be done to the person to make them release their personal power?*
A: A person had to be traumatized into separation of their natural connection to their heart, soul, body and sexual dignity. . A persons emotional centers for feeling must be exhausted/ drained thru pain to the point they are num to their feelings This process is done thru constant

The Black American Handbook for Survival

emotional invalidation, extreme physical abuse, rape, molestation, rape with sodomy, sexual torture and genital mutilation. A person loses their sense of belonging, safety, resulting in an intense fear of severe physical pain and suffering

Q: **What is rape?**

A: Rape is actions performed against the will of the person to rob or destroy a person's emotional balance of personal power thru violating the sacred sanctuaries of the body in a person. This action causes an emotional disturbance with-in a person, which results in a separation of the emotional self (feeling) to its connection to the heart, soul and to the physical world (intellect ego, body). The sacred trinity for unconscious connection to natural instinct is broken...

Consequently, a person's emotional ability to trust being intimate and receive intimacy is broken– without this bond a person cannot totally embrace his or her own humanness.

Q: **Why was it necessary to rape the children?**

A; Children operate in a state of natural instinct, this emotional nature is called innocence. Violating a child's innocence breaks a persons trust of their natural instincts. They live in an emotional state of denial and confusion. This process is the only way to break the child's trust with-in themselves of their natural emotional instincts, now in a state of internal confusion- they experience life with fear and become obedient to another master.

This form of violation starts a chain reaction: The male children as adults will have fear to- embrace their intimate nature, fear of unity, intense internalized fear with anger, isolation of inner self, they become sexual predators, irresponsible towards life – fear of commitment. Self hate.

The female children as adults will not be able to trust and embrace her intimate nature. She will no longer be able to have/ show compassion for her children or others. She will internalize her powerlessness, worthlessness, she, will lack self-esteem, she will provide but will not protect, stand for or emotionally nurture her children. She will no longer recognize her inherited connection to nature. The cycle of devastation starts.

Q: *What did the European colonist do after the children were broken into slavery to maintain there emotional bondage?*

A: Re-educate the children with the Patriarchal view of life instead of their ancestral Matriarchal view. Which is love for living things and the respect for the continuation of life. From the patriarchal view the children will now perceive their life as a process to live through instead of living for. There is no joy in living - joy of life is in death, their life condition is a punishment from God. God's grace belongs to man.

The Black American Handbook for Survival

God's chosen man is white. The enslaved Black American children were forced to believe that there life was a curse from the wrath of the White Father God. To be born black from the womb of the Anasazi woman was to be cursed into a placemen as a inferior person, you are a human beast of burden / animal, who has no heritage, culture, ancestral Legacy, identity, or belonging to nature. There is no compassion, care, concern, forgiveness, or meaningful purpose for his or her lives from God. The children who were raised ignorant of self were called Niggers

Q: ***What happened as a result from enslaving generations of Black American youth?***
A: Over generations of this constant killing off of the adult men, the dieing off of the ancestral Anasazi man, kidnapping and rape of the Young Anasazi (Black) American women of her children by European settlers the growing population of enslaved Black American children grew into adults. The European used the young adult males to capture and destroy their own people. The enslaved Black American people became the European mans human side kicks the young adults were as loyal to them as they would be to their own people, if they knew where they were. As adults they could only pass on fragmented information about their heritage, culture, language, and ancestral identity. The children of the slaves no longer recognized or respected whom they were and from whence they came. They hated their position in life and internalized

their inferiority from their color and hair as being a curse from their mother. The Black American female became the object for carnal sexual expression thru which sin is produced. She is unclean, un feminine, evil, destructive, inherently wicked, instinctual, and devoid of humanness. Her life became invisible and has no value '' There was no honor in their birth from her, so there was no reason to respect or protect the future generations

Q: **What is a Nigger?**
A: A nigger is a black person who is totality ignorant of self and its connection to humanity.

Q: **What does the term "Negro" mean?**
A: The European term "Negro" is: a captured and branded INDIAN/Anasazi (Black American) person who is now considered human property for sale. From 1492-1705 People who are not captured remain under the European classification as Indians. After 1705 the term Negro meant the same as the term Indian: Status to be enslaved ... However, it only applied to all colored people in America.

Q: **What is the definition of a" Negro as a slave?**
A; A person who 's life has been severely violated and traumatized to the point of numbness as a result from severe sexual, physical and emotional abuse. A person

The Black American Handbook for Survival

who is being denied all forms of natural freedom of humanity, and spiritual expression for feeling the joy of living. A person who lives in fear instead of the natural expression of the heart and soul.

Excerpt from
***The 17th Century Hostages,
Slaves, and Allies***

Some Indian girls were shipped to Bermuda to learn how to behave like Christian ladies, so that they could return to convert their tribes, but their lot was better than most. Large numbers of Indians from the Carolinas were enslaved and carried off to Bermuda, Barbados, and Jamaica. Governor Joseph West of South Carolina lined his pockets with the profits from this enterprise, and even induced Indians to capture other Indians so that their sale could add to his coffers. The situation deteriorated until, in 1693, the Cherokees urgently petitioned Thomas Smith, who was then governor of the South Carolina territory, to save them from the Catawbas, Shawnees, and Congarees, who had themselves been selling them profitably as slaves both to local planters and for shipment outside the country. But nothing was done to solve the problem permanently.

European opinion was still divided on how to treat the Indians. Although many Europeans continued to exploit the New

World's first inhabitants, they could not always do so with impunity. When Jacques de Denonville captured twenty-one Indians and took them to France "dressed in gorgeous French garments," as one eyewitness reported, other influential noblemen found this abduction so odious that when Louis de Frontenac succeeded Denonville as the governor of New France in 1689, they forced the "conqueror" to return these Indians to their native Canada. Despite this demonstration of sympathy for the Indians, Louis XIV continued to order Indian slaves to serve on his royal galleys. And so it went for the Indians, as capricious rulers in Europe alternated sympathy with exploitation in their dealings with them throughout the century."

Q: *Did Black American women have babies by their captors?*

A: No. Most Black female slaves did not live long enough to have a child. The constant violation of their bodies made it a hostile environment to bring forth life; just as most animals do not have children in captivity.

Q: *How did the Europeans infiltrate our Ancestral Black American bloodline?*

A: SURPRISE!!!!!! THROUGH allowing the MATING of WHITE WOMEN WITH STRONG YOUNG BLACK

BOYS. The Black American man became the European woman's sex toy!

The same problem Black American women have today: White women breeding with young, Black men. This is the process that will mutate and exterminate the full-blooded Black American people.

Q: Are today's Black Americans mixed with White blood?
A: Most of today's Black American people are not mixed with white blood. The European men tried to procreate with the Black American women for the purpose of birthright to the American land. This was not successful. Due to the genetics created by God - the Black American race is an older, stronger and superior genetic group of people than the Europeans.

Women of all races cannot mate with groups that are weaker than the original bloodline. It is called survival of the fittest. If there is a White Ancestor, it will be a European woman. This is the real secret behind breeding and who was doing the breeding.

Breeding was done thru European women to Black American men. This process of fornication with European women would start to harness the environmental genetics from the bloodline of the Anasazi (Black) American Women Nations Mound Builders in to the European Bloodline, ensuring that the European bloodline. would not die out while living in America, and allowing their future generations the ability to adapt easier to the environment of this land. This explains the glorification of White female beauty over the Black American female. Black American men are constantly being seduced by European images of women for mating.

Q: *Why do today's Black Americans have White sir names?*

A: The sir names were originally given to the captured Indians to represent the slave owner's property. The sir name had nothing to do with being of European Blood relation. All Indians were reduced to being boys and girls meaning, people who no longer had power to govern themselves. That is why Black American men despise being called "BOY".

Q: *Are all Black Americans descendants of imported Slave or Negro's?*

A: No. Most Black Americans people are not descendants of the people who were enslaved. However many of our people will have a descendant that might have been enslaved. The adoption of white sir names did not mean you were a slave; it was also used as a way to keep from being enslaved? Many Anasazi people embraced the European ideas and culture and betrayed their own people. Anasazi people adopted European words as names to protect themselves and the children. Also European people was constantly putting European names on the people regardless of there Ancestral name. Most Black Americans had two names. One was their Indian name and the other was there European identity.
Remember Negro was applied to all the Anasazi people called Indians To maintain your Indian identity meant to be betrayed, hunted and killed as animals or enslaved.
Some European words that were made into sir names are: Green Woods, White, Brown, Tree, and Bird, just to name a few.

The Black American Handbook for Survival

Why did many Black Americans CHOSE to accept living as Negro's?

As a Negro a person can abandon their spiritual responsibility for life, nature, and the condition of life for the future generations. People can exploit themselves and others unconsciously, indulge in sexual hedonism, selfishness, isolation, and individualism. The consequence to this thinking is a person develops a deep seated sense of powerlessness, fear, guilt, and self hate

The person who chose to become a Negro- in essence is a person who chose to live as a heathen, violating all of life joys of living, for immediate carnal pleasure and material satisfaction.

"A Heathen"
or
Savage= a person who lacks natural instincts

As Long as Black Americans Abandon their responsibility to the future generations and do not recognize
what Exploitation for carnal pleasure, and control does to their young adults and children.
The future generations will be trapped in mental
and emotional bondage \they will always be considered as
American Heathens called Negro's

The Black American Handbook for Survival

Dianne Flecther – Knowas tribe –Indian slave called Negro

All Black American People are the remaining Lineages of the Anasazi People of North America (The Original Indians) Regardless if you perceive your ancestors arrived by land or by sea.

They were the Anasazi People who were enslaved and robbed of their Identity, Heritage, civilization, culture, and land.

The Black American Handbook for Survival

UNDERSTANDING THE UNITED STATES OF = VS. AMERICA

Understanding the Black American Position Today

Q: *Where did the African story, "The Middle Passage", come from?*

A: Over the generations, the Indigenous youth needed a sense of connection to humanity other than the European ideal of being an enslaved / conquered people. During the sixties, a movement started to resurrect Negro American Self Esteem. "Our" well assimilated / educated elite found a commonality with the West African people's experience of European occupation/ slavery as being similar to ours, as well as marketability (a way to make money) to the Negro American and U.S., as a way for Young Indigenous people to recognize their humanity without rocking the MATRIX, WHICH SUPPORTS THE wealth of the NEGRO ELITE.

Many Indigenous Americans found a sense of pride / heritage with their connection to Africa and adopted the identity./ heritage. This new sense of pride allowed Indigenous Americans to abandon their real identity and responsibility for themselves as a collective / race AND allowed Indigenous leadership to abandon their RESPONSIBILITY. Towards the struggle for the people with the issues of –recognition, respect and self-reliance in there own land.

However, Adopting another race and heritage does not make you a person of that race or heritage, nor does it erase your responsibility to your own heritage and race. The difference between Indigenous American people and people from West Africa . and the Caribbean IS THE West African people did not forget the value of their heritage / identity and fought to regained their independence and self-recognition.

Through the 21st Century – Vol. I

In the 1980's, Jesse Jackson promoted to the Indigenous Anasazi people of North America called Indians, mulattos, Negroes, to totally abandon their truth and IDENTIFY THEMSEVES AS enslaved foreigners (foreign subject gated people) called "African-Americans." As Afro- Americans the only connection / recognition indigenous Anasazi people have to there heritage and homeland is chains and boats. from the middle of nowhere.......

Note: the original passage was transporting people downstream to different plantations took one to two weeks- not across the ocean. The assimilated Educational institutions fought for U.S. funding to promote this false connection to Africa (lie) be taught to the future generations...

Q: *Why are Black Americans educated to look towards Africa for their identity?*

A: During the past 35 years, Indigenous young Americans have been assimilated / educated into a new concept.. The new identity concept will maintain the invisibility to the Ancestral connection to their Anasazi heritage and birthright as the original undisputed owners of the land that the United Corporate States had STOLEN from! .This will allow Black American youth to FEEL totally dis-placed. REJECTED, and powerless to change what happens to them or their children. This concept will allow the future generations to accept their powerlessness and be Proud to SURVIVE being enslaved instead of fighting for self-determination and real freedom. They will internalize their placement on this land as sharecroppers and continue to assimilate into a culture

The Black American Handbook for Survival

and system that express to them that they are not wanted and they have no where to go. This will allow the European people to escalate the perpetuation of systematic domestication and perpetual ethnocide of them as a people

Q: *Why wasn't I taught about my Indian Ancestors and their experience fighting for their humanity and freedom in school?*

A: Because Indigenous American youth could use their education to develop ways of regaining their Ancestral freedom as a people and to restore balance to their homeland, stopping the destruction of the resources that feed and maintain their future generations.

- This means: stopping corporations like *"Home Depot"* from making money on the destruction of the fertile forest. Also, if the Indigenous American people would stop supporting the destruction of their homeland, this country would be in a different place today and Indigenous Americans would have more power over their self determination in it.

Anasazi / Indian /- Black American people
would no longer perceive themselves worthless=powerless

Q: *How does the European educational system maintain a enslave mentality among today's Indigenous Americans?*

A: By omitting the true story of how the early colonialists acquired the land thru slavery, the purpose of slavery,, by omitting the true racial identity of the largest group of Indigenous American people, termed Indian, as Negro/brown/black invisible. AND BY FUNDING ANY ORGANIZATION OR EDUCATIONL INSTITUTION THAT PROMOTES European agendas.

Originally the Christian American church and Negro colleges was developed to assimilate/condition Indigenous people into compliance thru adopting European attitudes about themselves as their primary value system-.(which is Human property.) The result creates an inferiority complex within the psyche of the REAL American children.(their life has no value) As adults, they internalize in their heart that they owe someone else for their right to belong in humanity. and despise their heritage identity and race. instead of understanding the land in which they stand is their inherited birthright, which is being exploited and trashed by other races of people..

They accept their position as sharecroppers in a foreign land

Q: **How did the United Corporate States steal your homeland and birth heritage?**

A: First, by renaming your identity from Indian to Negro in the Early 1700's.. Selling the 14th Amendment to the Indigenous people to become a part of the United States with privileges of citizenship that are not the same as rights......

The Black American Handbook for Survival

Q: *Are today's Black Americans citizens of the United States?*
A: No; not actually. The citizenship is voluntary and comes with a heavy price. After the United States civil war, the United States had to work with the Anasazi people in order to form the country. Concessions were made to help form the new alliance and country. The Fourteenth Amendment was adopted to allow all the people from the Anasazi Nations (Negroes) under the privilege of citizenship, but not the right of citizenship. This illusion of privilege as rights came with an exchange to the United States, a land trust from Indian/ Anasazi people .to their lands. Today all lands that belong to the Nations of Anasazi people under United States control are public land meaning lands belonging to the Anasazi/black American people However, the Anasazi Nations did not know they were giving their heritage and lands away. Nor did they concede as a conquered race of people. This misconception took generations to be implemented.

Q: *What does "Privilege to" mean?*
A: A **privilege** is a right granted on conditions.
A **right** is an unconditional inheritance.

Example:
A Landlord has the *"right;"*
a Tenant has the *"privilege."*

All Black Americans are Public Citizens, meaning Anasazi descendants to American land that is in trust

Through the 21st Century – Vol. I

Spiritual Understanding

to the United States; as long as Anasazi/Black Americans consider themselves as citizens.

In exchange the United States will recognize and give you (the Black American) the <u>privilege</u> of acting as a "Private Citizen" but, not a <u>right</u> of a Private Citizen, as in "We The People".

Q: *What did the Indigenous Americans unknowingly release for the recognition of the privilege of being Public Citizens?*

A: In exchange, the Nations of Anasazi people stopped their fight for self-determination, ownership of their homeland, heritage, culture, ancestry, and viability of their future generations.

Q: *Can Black Americans receive reparations from the United States for their enslavement on their land?*

A: <u>No</u>! The XIV (14) (1868) Amendment of the Constitution of the United States, Section 4 prohibits reparations with the following:

"But neither the <u>United States nor any State shall assume or pay any dept or obligation</u> incurred in aid of insurrection or rebellion against the United States, or LOSS OR EMANCIPATION OF ANY SLAVE, BUT ALL SUCH DEPTS, OBLIGATIONS AND CLAIMS SHALL BE HELD ILLEGAL AND VOID."

The Black American Handbook for Survival

(PLEASE, read and understand The Constitution of the United States. - The United States Congress cannot make an Amendment that can go against the Constitution of the United States!)

Q: *When did I sign my rights away?*

A: This is automatically done at birth to Black American women by the United States; when your mother receives a child's birth certificate and social security card. However as though most Black American Women do not sign the Birth certificates. Most Black Americans have not signed their birthrights away, nor has they claimed them.. Black Americans are conditioned to be sharecroppers on their land, for the use and maintenance of European comfort and control. However, this position is totally voluntary.

Q; *Why must racism exist in America?*

A; Racism will always exist in America as long as Black Americans exist in America, because all Black Americans represent the original American Indians / Anasazi people who belong in America and have a right to belong and live freely with self determination and national recognition on this land. As long as Black American people exist in America, the United States does not have World Rights nor sovereignty to the land or in the land. The United States remains as a foreign occupation of people who are controlling the lands of another race of people. The same as when the English controlled the South African people

Spiritual Understanding

Q: *What Does the United States have to do to completely inherit (STEAL) the civilization / lands of the Anasazi people of North America from their descendants called Black Americans today?*

A: The United States must institute an agenda for Ethnic Cleansing that can systematically undermine the mental, spiritual and physical well-being; which will reduces the regenerative numbers of Anasazi Americans over generations to a point of non-existence.

Q: *What is "genocide?"*

A: It is the coordinated and planned annihilation of a national, religious, or racial group by a variety of actions aimed at undermining the foundation essential to the survival of the group as a group. An attack on political and social institutions, culture, language, national feeling, religious practices and beliefs, and the economic existence of the group constitutes **genocide**. Even non-lethal acts undermine the liberty, dignity, and personal security of members of a group, if they contribute to weakening the group's vitality. This includes acts of **ethnocide:** the process of destroying a culture without the killing of its bearers (i.e., slavery, police brutality, poverty, foster care, just to name a few).

Q: *How is this agenda effectively implemented?*

A: **First**, and foremost: Keep the Anasazi/ Black American man (his physical and mental force)

The Black American Handbook for Survival

embracing the Patriarchal mentality. Instead of recognizing or respecting his life force in the Anasazi / Black American woman; as his center (his heart) and their regenerative power in manifesting through the Anasazi/Black American child. (the soul). The Anasazi man must be seduced into embracing the illusion that he is an independent individual, the dominant/ controlling center for the force of life of his race: The Anasazi man must not recognize that his renewed power/force is through his children.

The Anasazi American population needs the physical, mental and emotional force of the children with the direction from the wisdom of the Anasazi woman and Anasazi man to correct the wrongs of the past. Only an Anasazi American woman with an Anasazi American man can reproduce and restore the race to its complete wholeness.

The woman produces children and emotionally nurtures, the man gives mental direction and fortitude. Without this cohesion between the Indigenous Man and Woman, today's Anasazi/ indigenous Man will never harness the power needed to overcome their bondage. The indigenous American Man must be kept mentally and spiritually unconscious to his natural relationship to the expression of life, inherited belonging, and humanity , so he will continue to seek separation and abandon his responsibility to maintain the production that support and protect the Indigenous woman, children, and preserve viable living conditions for the future generations.

Through the 21st Century – Vol. I

As a Result

The Anasazi American man unconsciously exploits his own to become a destructive force to himself and to his race.

Leaving the Anasazi American woman abandoned and without the support and protection form the Anasazi man of her sacred life force . The European people can infiltrate, disrupt and control the sacred rights and natural process of the Anasazi American woman's to replenish her bloodlines thru her fertility; and to systematically reduce the survival of what is produced from the Black American woman's womb. (camouflaged as a Black woman's need for birth control; thru the fear of lack and over population.. (Forgetting the truth: All life is ordained by God not By man, and all Anasazi women have a duty first to regenerate their bloodlines on their lands given to them by God) The illusion of lack , poverty, pain and suffering allows a woman to abandon her responsibility to procreate for the survival of her race in exchange for fulfilling all of her personal desires and, as protection from the destructive behavior of Anasazi men who now feel that it is their right to violate and exploit women as sexual objects.

. The Black American woman loses control of her right to her body and, her right to bring forth life in a natural process. She must now submit to the pain and suffering resulting from the violation from the European man's intrusion upon her body while bringing forth life. *(Gynecology, Obstetrics was developed from this violation of Anasazi American women while giving birth for control of the Black American people's regenerative life force.*

The Black American Handbook for Survival

In order for the children to survive, the abandoned Young Anasazi American women with child is forced to assimilate their child into systems that maintain the European's control, de-moralization, rape and bondage of the Anasazi American future generations in their homeland.

Second: Break down the Anasazi peoples natural body immune systems that maintains their life longevity AND fertility (this is done by stripping the melanin from natural foods with chemical processing; example; sugar is a nutrient Anasazi people used for thousands of years, the chemical processing of natural sugar into white sugar, changes sugar from being a nutrient for the pineal gland that allows our people to converse with nature into a poison that stops our connection, addictive, and depletes our energy.. as well as the promotion of homogenized milk as part of a required food group; when cow's are not indigenous to America nor did Anasazi people ever drink milk from any animal to get protein. Animal protein other than fresh water fish actually breaks down the life longevity for Anasazi people. . liquor; the replacement of drugs over natural remedies, etc.).

These examples are just the tip of the Iceberg for all the distortions that are being implemented on the Anasazi people towards their permanent extinction form their lands

Third: To keep Anasazi Americans contained in sterile deforested environments with government controlled housing and community development. Called ghettos. Ghettos were developed in Europe by Hitler to contain for extermination the European Jewish people and extract their wealth. These ghettoes in the United States are called Projects or

Through the 21st Century – Vol. I

Spiritual Understanding

reservations for some Southwestern indigenous people. the result is the indigenous people of America will become ignorant over generations of her/ his connection to their land and how to live in their Natural environment.. The indigenous people will lose valuable information to sustain and protect themselves. The Indigenous people of North America will no longer be able to operate independently in their natural environment.

Ultimately – To develop the technology that can find, extract or duplicate the Anasazi American genetic (DNA) from the after-birth (the placenta) of the Anasazi American child from the mother's womb; the inherited connection to the natural environment of North America and infuse it into the European gene.

This will allow the Europeans to harness the fertility, genetic history and physical superiority that are transferred from the Anasazi American woman to child. The European woman will be able to produce and replenish the European genetically-altered generations on this land without requiring the Anasazi American racial type or the Anasazi American man.

The New European Goal

THE ULTIMATE RAPE: Black American on the inside and White (European) on the outside. European technology is about to successfully brake and change the natural life force that governs the continuance of the specialty and divinity of the natural cycle of human life, the environment and to exterminate the chosen races living on this planet.

Over time, the Anasazi American woman and her people will become distorted relics of **his-story**. The European man will successfully steal the inherited genetics and replace the Black man as the new superior race of all human species...

The Anasazi American man as we know him to be will die out as being fickle, mentally incompetent and, physically obsolete.

- **The NEW MANKIND OF THE 21ST**
- **CENTURY...**
   This is The NEW WORLD ORDER!

Q: ***Why is it important for the Black man and woman to unite, rebuild trust , self-respect and return to the ways of their ancestral heritage and family***

A: It is the only way the Anasazi people will be able to survive thru the 21st Century.

The main focus of the European race is to destroy the future reproduction of the full-blooded Black American people (termed Indians) bloodlines. Over the generations, European devastation and destruction has taken a toll on the heritage, culture, and bloodlines of the Indigenous American people called Black Americans.

As long as the Anasazi Man and woman do not understand and respect the importance of unity with each other, the race will not be strong enough to maintain its survival. The Brown/ Red race will die. It is imperative that the European collective break up Indigenous American families and maintain attitudes that promote exploitation, dis-respect, betrayal, and irresponsibility towards each other, will keep the family unit from ever having unity. Only this procedure will guarantee the complete extermination of the ORIGINAL KEEPERS and owners of this land called North America.

The Anasazi American Mound Builders

Excerpt from George Catlin 1841

" Letters and Notes on the North American Indians"

" So long as the present systems of trade and whisky-selling is tolerated, there is little hope. I have closely studied Indian character in its native state, and also in secondary form (as Negro's) along our (captured) frontiers .I have seen it in every phase, and although there are many noble instances to the contrary of whom I personally acquainted with-yet the greater men have been beaten into a sort of civilization (heathens) which is very far from being civilized by examples of good and moral men. They surrender their land and their fair hunting grounds too the enjoyment of their enemies, their bones are dug up and strewed about the fields or labeled in our museums.

For the Christian, there is enough, I am sure, in the character, conditions, and history for these unfortunate people, to engage his sympathies. For the Nation (United States) there is an unrequited account of sin and injustice that sooner or later will call for National retribution. For the American citizen, who live everywhere proud of their growing wealth and their luxuries, .over the bones of these poor fellows there is a lingering terror for reflecting minds.

Our mortal bodies must soon take their humble places with their red/brown brethren, under the same glebe; to appear and stand at last with guilt's shivering conviction, amid the myriad ranks of accusing spirits at the final day resurrection.
"

(Please note; Catlin had no love for the Indian)

Spiritual understanding of the Black American Holocaust

Many Indigenous Americans today internalize their position in the world as people who are co-dependant upon others to sustain us as long as we keep them happy. (similar to children) Indigenous Americans have accepted their position as being powerless to make effective change in their lives that will change the future. As a result we accept our place as being the victim instead of the victor. However, Indigenous Americans fail to take serious stock in honoring the resiliency of themselves as people. They are still hanging on even though they are extremely crippled as a people thru this 500-year holocaust. Indigenous American people have withstood tremendous tribulation on their own soil and will have to endure / overcome a lot more to keep their future generations alive. What cripples Indigenous Americans the most is the lack of knowledge for their ancestral heritage. And respect to understanding the adherence to Natural law that empowers them. Today's generations are blind to the understanding / power with-in the Natural Laws, which can protect and empower them or enable their victimization. It is time that Indigenous Americans give understanding/ following Natural Law some serious thought…

Q; **Why is understanding and respecting Natural Law so important?**
A: Without the understanding of Natural Law a person/ group/ race cannot tell the difference between the truth and a lie. Reality or false illusion.

Q; **What are some of the spiritual lessons to be learned from this holocaust of our people?**
A: Our ancestor as well as our people today must learn, that when you have a race of people who has no respect, compassion, honor, care or concern for human life = no

love for life. You do not expect them to change by honoring them with life.. You honor life by setting boundaries that maintain your honor, care, compassion respect and concern for yourself. =Self-love. IT IS NOT A GROUPS RESPONSIBILITY TO HONOR ANY GROUP WHO HAS NO RESPECT FOR THE GROUP. Indigenous Americans must realize their power is in working and creating life systems not in the consumption and destruction of life systems. That is why our Ancestral land was so rich in Natural (life) abundance, Only when we operate in our power with-in natural law can we overcome all in balance and disharmony.

Q; *What did the European man offer the Indigenous American man that put the people and future generations into bondage?*

A; **1.** A mental attitude change that supported the disrespect and invalidation towards the feminine spiritual principal and power that governs life. The contributions of women, children and the environment that supports human life.
2. A way for the Black man to receive temporary physical, material gratification from the illusion of power without responsibility through exploitation.
3. Escaping the responsibility towards their contribution for the production that is need to support, protect the women, children, and the environment which maintains their freedom in life.

The price paid…….Loss of mental and spiritual power.

The results: *Slavery—Exploitation, Consumption and destruction of the systems that support the life of the Anasazi/ Black American people in all forms.*

.

The Black American Handbook for Survival

A Spiritual truth: A man is no more that the life from which he came. Whatever the condition of life for the mother, will be the condition of life for the son (man).

Q: *What did women do after they felt abandoned by the man, that maintains the perpetual powerlessness of the future generations?*
A: Anasazi women lost respect for and abandon the Anasazi man consciously. She stop promoting values of the ancestral heritage that empowered the children spiritually (Example: A person who has nothing to stand for will having nothing to die for, as a result his essence becomes useless.) and respect for the importance of maintaining the emotional, mental, spiritual viability that comes from the belonging and knowledge of Heritage to the future generations.

Q: *What do women have to learn?*
A: Life is ordained by the Holy Sprit not by man? Regardless how man may abandon women. Woman is the spiritual portal/ vehicle that creates human life, nurtures life, and nature, you are love, and all life is centered around you. As long as women sustain love for themselves in following what is in-herited in her heart, no man/ race can conquer you.

Indigenous American women can correct the wrongs of the past for they hold the key to the future in their womb, and thru children. Women are the first teacher of the children and it is up to women to focus on creating a community to raise the children in ways that correct the past. As long as women teach the children as children, respect for their Heritage (women, nature, life,) and themselves, the wrongs of the past will not manifest into the future. Women can change the future as quick as the blink of an eye.

Through the 21st Century – Vol. 1

Spiritual Understanding

As long as Indigenous American Mothers condone abandonment of the Lineages or children by their sons., Young women will always be abandoned with children.
Remember.
All children represent the perpetuation of the lineages into the future. All children are born into two extended families Young Indigenous women must realize, the reason women do not have any husbands, is because the generations of Elders women before them abandoned their responsibility to raise their sons to be conscious men nor do they want to take responsibility for development of the future bloodlines.

As long as young mother s continue to make the mistake of the recent elders and choose to be caretakers of their children instead of raising the children to be conscious and responsible men and women.
Our future generations are doomed to be mentally, spiritually, emotionally weak and poor.. Living with poor states of mind such as fear, ignorance, lack, and stagnation.
Indigenous American women must understand it is their responsibility to develop the consciousness in the boys and girls.. Anasazi mothers must return to ways of our Ancestral Heritage and the conscious perpetuation of nurturing/ educating the Bloodlines. This is their first purpose, Instead of embracing the false illusion promoted from European ethos of being self-centered, selfish and emotionally consumed with material illusion for self worth...

Q; What do Indigenous American people have to do to heal themselves?
Realize they cannot serve two masters. First, Stop exploiting thru betrayal their natural nature and embrace with respect their imitate relationships between each other. This will allow trust to develop.. Recognize, learn, atone. and forgive themselves for the mistakes of the past. Learn and Return to the respecting the ways of our true ancestors- who represented the best of

The Black American Handbook for Survival

humanity. We must re-learn to trust, honor respect, care, concern and compassion for each other FIRST. Release the illusion of fear that following your heart will bring you pain instead of fulfilling joy. Return to standing for and following their real Ancestral Heritage. The healing is instant.

Q: ***Is money the answer?***
A: It is a part of the solution, but not the solution itself. The solution is what Indigenous Americans do as a collective with their money is the answer to re-building there future. Example: if every Indigenous American sent $1 to the black farmers $2 to funds that supported the development of educational programs for our children to learn their heritage and Natural Law. We would be able to produce enough food to support our own markets. This is just a few things a small investment to us from ourselves could do..

For more understanding look for the volume the Spiritual Understanding and Advantages of the Black American Holocaust.

PRAYER FOR " OUR" PEOPLE

Holy spirit help us trust in the spirit within us
Help us trust the goodness in our people
Let the illusions that hold us back as individuals and as a society now disappear.
Show us a light at the center of our pain
Show us a light at the center of our disillusionment
Release the fear to forgive my brother
Release the fear to love my sister
For truly we are reborn or we die together.
Where I see guilt- show me innocence
Where I see mistakes- Let me see change to focus on efforts for good.
Let us have a new sense of purpose
Lead us back to our Nature
Let us return to our brilliance
Revive in us our passion
Let us return to our depth and nobility
Restore us to our beauty.
Our people have suffered enough in coming to this point.
With this prayer may unity begin again- having released the past seeking from the Holy Spirit a new path forward.
We place both past and future in the grace of the Holy Spirit.
We are " One" Graced by the Holy Spirit
May our People remain so forever.
We are the light- and light of truth we shall remain
A men

The Black American Handbook for Survival

CONCLUSION

IT is unfortunate that our elders since 1868 chose to integrate into and adopt attitudes of a society and culture that will only support their self-destruction. Indigenous Black Americans hold MOST of the blame for their destruction. Black American people will have to realize that there is no power without responsibility. , Indigenous Black Americans as a collective have become quite proficient at "passing the buck" or " dumping" as they say, and not taking responsibility for re-building the foundation that would ensure the survival for the future generations by producing what is necessary to stop the actions within their community that facilitate the destruction of their heritage, culture, genocide of their own people and homeland. Each generation has received less knowledge from the previous generation, as a result each generation has become more ignorant about their understanding of self (enslaved) than the generation before them.

Today, because of the mistakes of our recent elders, Indigenous Black American people have little knowledge of themselves. We have become products of a "Slave History"; a Euro centric world view, which by definition, cannot be developmental or inspirational. This history, for the most part, has been written, disseminated, and taught by the sons and daughters of the people who continue to exploit, raped America of its people and wealth. Who ancestors has literally, sprinkled Anasazi Americans around the world. They, while doing this, developed (created) in their politics, science, arts, economics, education, and religion a rationale for the destruction of Indigenous American people. The effective results of this Euro centric rationale provided the

Conclusion

intellectual and moral basis for Euro centric control of the new world.

All the blame should not fall on the shoulders of the European race. This discourse is not intended to continue creating hate towards the Europeans or other foreigners who have come to this land to create opportunities thru exploitation in America against the indigenous people. Remember, People who come here from other lands are people who are not willing to take responsibility for creating positive change for balance and harmony in their God Given lands. (*Many foreigners ignore this truth and may need to be reminded of this truth when they dis-respect indigenous people)* All people regardless of what illusion they believe and create, does not change the natural laws of truth. The law of cause and effect is always in full force whether we choose to honor it or not. This rule of universal govern ship is applicable to people, genders, and races. The rule is called KARMA. It is not necessary for Anasazi people/ race to keep looking for the European race to effect a change and give them back anything. It will be up to the Anasazi American people to learn from the lessons of the past. There is nothing given to you without and exchange for something. (In other words THERE IS NOTHING FOR FREE including your spiritual homeland. God gave your homeland to you, and you are held responsible to it and for it. it is not the responsibility of the European race to educate the Anasazi American people about their experience, natural environment, heritage or support them and their future generations It is the

The Black American Handbook for Survival

responsibility of the Black American people to produce what is necessary to support, maintain there identity, heritage, hisstory, their mental, spiritual, and physical well being and support. (food, .clothing, electricity, housing, fuel, etc.)

May the light

Of truth save the beautiful

Black American people

from extinction...

Today it has become convenient for Black Americans to look for avenues to avoid the issues that plague our people and stay invisible to our "truth". This allows us, as a collective, to be apathetic, selfish, irresponsible and receive personal benefits from encouraging civil enslavement rather than to take responsibility for improving the condition of our lives and future generations. Unfortunately, because of the adoption of this growing attitude, Indigenous Americans over the last 500 years have **"LOST"** the direction of their future (the children), their knowledge of their **past (HERITAGE, IDENITITY), their present (PRODUCTION FROM THEIR HOMELAND) AS A direct consequence from Avoiding TAKING SERIOUS RESPONSIBILITY FOR PRODUCING THE SUPPORT FOR THEIR LIFE IN THEIR HOMELAND.** . Anasazi American leadership has exploited (sold out) all the Grace God has given them. Regardless how the Anasazi people choose to avoid this responsibility to our selves, the lesson we will have to learn

Conclusion

is that " You can not serve two masters…. When Black American people chose to put their energy looking with-in themselves into producing the structural support they need for themselves and families from the ground up. Only then will they have a sense of power. Instead of trying to avoid doing the work and facing the challenges that are presented. All Anasazi people will find out " the holy spirit will never give a people a challenge they can not overcome. It is the false perception that is the key to all defeat. The Challenge that face Anasazi American is" Who will be your Master the Holy Spirit or Man. .The Anasazi American people have to return the truth Man is not the power over life, he is a supporter of life and nature. When we releases this horrible perception we will be given the power to produce and re-create a civilization greater than the one of our ancestors and never be enslaved again. Our fears of persecution from the European people will fade. It will not be necessary to kill or harm them or participate in any forms of death to other people or Nations We will stand strong regardless of what actions is taken against us. This is the true message Martin Luther King Jr. was expressing to the Negro American People "Our power is within our love for life and Nature. Once the Anasazi American people embraces this truth and take action towards self-production from nature **our mental bondage** is over. When All Anasazi women start to embrace, respect each other's healing power with-in our intimate nature. This is the power that **will heal the emotional wounds** of her people. . Stop being self centered and selfish.

The Black American Handbook for Survival

When Black American people return to respecting life, nature, and all that produces and supports their life, **this holocaust is over.**

THE SOLUTION

Today Black American must understand that they can't ignore the position they are in and must seriously look at what it will take to give our people a chance to live on this planet in the future. If Anasazi People continue to ignore their \God given grace and perpetuate the attitudes from this foreign culture, Anasazi people will not survive thru the 21st Century. It is imperative for today's Anasazi people to search out, recognize, reclaim, their ancestral heritage, identity, and self worth.

It's SIMPLY a CHANGE OF ATTITUDE—

From CONSUMPTION (destruction) **to CONSTRUCTION** (production):
(<u>**A** return to our God given position of maintaining and protecting life on this planet</u>). Remember, we are the last decedents of the "Planet Keepers".

If Indigenous Black Americans chose, as a collective, to use their ability to respond with action towards regaining autonomy of their lives, and start to embrace, their inherited ability to produce and cultivate life within Nature. they will have everything to supports their lives, the genocide of their people and the planet would stop <u>immediately;</u> generations would be saved from extinction and the homeland restored to its full splendor of EDEN. Only Today's **Black Americans using their Indigenous heritage have the power to change and <u>stop</u> the mass destruction of the planet and "OUR" homeland.** Let go of the illusion of fear of persecution and victimization; from the European people. **Take action**

towards the future of life. It is up to us. Black Americans must trust the truth in natural Law, which represents God.

Reality is everything that is in union.
Illusion is anything that creates separation.

Black Americans will have to start working instead of talking about the dynamics that surround our lives and say " All right, no matter how they were created, no matter what systems was developed to maintain it, it is really important that I take responsibility personally for living only in a unified place, only being alive in reality" The presence of life is always greater than death.

When Black Americans embrace their Anasazi heritage as indigenous people and commit themselves to support, protect and live for life, instead of finding ways to ignore their identity and escape responsible action towards the continuation of life, there is no need to fear death.

The power of life is always greater than death. Fear is what shuts down the power of life's protection. When the young Adults of Anasazi / Black Americans are clear about their indigenous identity, then what we show in the light of day will take on new power as well as new beauty. Then, and only then do we begin to understand and change politics. As long as we focus on the Euro-Centered view of the world, which does not represent the truth or our true base of knowledge, and try to wield power of the kind only known to them, we will remain in the weaker, confused, enslaved position.

As Black American people especially Women as indigenous people remember they are the guardians for this land and planet, then the false Kings will wake up at last and honor our presence, the spirits will open the gates. We as a people won't storm the walls of power, the walls will melt away, then and

The Black American Handbook for Survival

only then will they set a table for us to feast instead of tossing us bones. The entire world will recognize and respect us when we respect and recognize ourselves. This Holocaust is over.

"We are the 'Sleeping Giant'
--- It's time to Wake Up!"

All Black Americans owe it to themselves to embrace, respect and learn more about the heritage of their ancestors who are the Anasazi people and their civilization of American Mound Builders called Indians of North, Central and South America.

Today all the races in the world admire our ancestral Legacy heritage. Our tremendous Ancestral heritage, as the Nubians, Egyptians, Hebrews (JEWS) and Indians of the America's, is one that all Black Americans should be proud to stand for and by. Embracing our true heritage, will give all people called Black Americans a sense of belonging, a respectable placement, as a viable contributor to and in humanity, family unity, self esteem, dignity, respect towards each other and the power to return back to the attitudes and principles of our ancestors.

Today people who claim our heritage are not of our blood *however*; **they do cherish, respect and follow** some of **the ancestor's traditions and principles** that created the greatest civilization on earth for over 12,000 years.

Solution

All Black Americans should embrace Indigenous American customs with respect and learn more about the American story they dare not tell. It is time for Black Americans to take stock in and respect us for the tremendous ancestral heritage of whom we truly are THE ANASAZI Nations of Mound Builders THE ORGINAL PEOPLE OF AMERICIA and have every right to recognize. It is time to learn from the mistakes of the past and reclaim the future of the race.

To help learn more about our forgotten knowledge and story the following editions will be available soon:

The Children's Book of Heritage
The Stolen legacy of the Black American People.
The un-told story about slavery in America
The Hidden contributions of Today's Black American Anasazi ancestors and their civilizations (children Books)
"Legacy of the Heart" Spiritual Lessons from The Black American Holocaust."
The Black American Church- - it's agenda   Past, Present, and Future.
And many more!!!!!!!!!

The Black American Handbook for Survival

The REAL Respectable TERM FOR TODAYS BLACK AMERICAN IDENITITY!!!!

is

I AM
INDIGENOUS
MEANING

I CAME BEFORE Columbus

The original Indian

I belong here

Use the **term Indigenous**

Instead of Black

Indigenous American

Instead of Afro- American

Through the 21st Century – Vol. I

Action Plan

-To re-claim "OUR ANCESTRAL Indigenous (Black) American Identity and Heritage:

First - Indigenous (Black) Americans must recognize their true Ancestral identity, their connection to life, their contribution to humanity, dignity, and self-determination in their homeland.

Second – reclaim our heritage, culture, and tribal identities, as the Anasazi people of North America. the five civilized tribes and others that created the Nations of Mound builders civilization. and recognition from the World Council Court in Geneva, Switzerland with a seat, as the indigenous people of North America. All Black Americans should be recognized in the charter of the United Nations, the Universal declaration of human rights and international human rights law and protection.

Third - All Black Americans should take the responsibility to make sure all our people know how to read and write. Black Americans should take full responsibility of the education, up bringing, training and well being of their children.

Fourth- stop encouraging the youth of the Black American Mound Builders descendants participation in the United States Armed Forces for any reason *other than* to protect their homeland from invasion of another foreign power.

Fifth- Start to collect the remaining fragments of our ancestral knowledge from our elders that cultivate our inherited ability to create with nature. (i.e. Agriculture, construction, fishing, ect)

The Black American Handbook for Survival

The Geneva Project
Reclaiming our Humanity

What is the purpose?

1. To Reclaim our Rights to Life, Humanity, Self-Determination, Heritage, Culture, Homeland, Resources, and Rights to stop the COLLECTION AND WHOLESALING OF GENETIC MATERIAL FROM Indigenous BLACK AMERICAN CHILDREN FOR the genetic benefit and profit of another race of people (i.e. the United States and their Affiliate Bio-engineering corporations).

2. World recognition of the Black Americans as the Indigenous North American People.

3. Letter to All Nations asking forgiveness for any and all harm done to other nations of people from Indigenous Black Americans' participation from being under the control of the United States.

What can I do?

1. **First Step - Find family names in the tribal appendix following this chapter.** Fill out and Sign the Geneva project petitions with all family members and mail . Time is of the essence.

2. **Second Step -** Tell someone about the book and share the information. Ask your elders for their stories....

3. **Third Step -** Go to libraries; research all you can. There are many fragments waiting to be rediscovered about our Heritage. Look under the heading of North

American Indians or Amerindians. Do not be fooled by the cover.

Where can I find more information about my Indian Ancestors called the Mound Builders?

At the library under Native Americans or First Americans or Mound Builders. Have fun. Learn the truth about your Indian Blood, Culture and Heritage.

Tell the Children. This will stop the pain in the future.

Go to Pow-wow's. Don't get upset if you don't see people dressed looking like you. **_Remember this is your stolen heritage._** The people who walk in your ancestor's shoes have maintained some of the beauty of your Ancestral culture. Respect it. Learn it. BE proud to be an Indian. Be proud to be a Black American. You have a Legacy that is greater than all the Legacies on the earth.

Black Americans also have a Holocaust that is greater than all the suffering on the earth. Now it is time to heal and triumph with victory from all the Nations of the Earth. Don't be afraid for all the people of the World are waiting for the Black American people to sit at the throne of humanity once again.

4. **Fourth Step** - Learn more or sponsor a ***Hidden Heritage Lecture.***

5. **Fifth Step** - Thank God for this Grace of knowledge and Start healing and grounding by attending a Sacred Journeys Retreat Watch how God will lead you on your path of Awaking your heart to your highest purpose for this life...

- *Watch and see!!!*

The Black American Handbook for Survival

For your petition

call **1-877-571-9788**
email: genevaproject@BlackAmericanHandbook.com

*Experience Your Ancestral Heritage
Healing of the Heart and Family Bloodlines.*

Sacred Ancestral Journeys
Healing of the Heart Retreats.....

Sacred Journey Retreats starts the healing process for reconnecting the psyche and heart, this allows Anasazi / Black American people to recognize, reclaim, embrace the natural healing power with-in our intimate nature and DNA. These sacred ceremonies of our Ancestors starts healing the family bloodlines from the traumas of the past, allowing a person/ family to understand and change the behavioral conditioning from bondage that perpetuate separation, inner fragmentation disillusionment. and pain.

The sacred ancestral ceremonies are performed on weekends from March thru October in the Appalachian mountains of Western North Carolina and the Tuckessegee River. All indigenous people are welcome. Group / Family / Church rates available. For more information and dates contact:

Sacred Journeys
1-866-395-3262 or 1-877-571-9788
Email: sacredjourneys@blackamericanhandbook.com

Find your Ancestral Nation

Cherokee
Chickasaws
Choctaws,
Creeks,
Seminoles

Tribal Surnames

As though all Indians are Negro = Black, I have included the lists of freedmen Indians. This partial List of English sir names of enslaved people from the Southeastern Nations of Black American Mound Builders.

The Northern nations of tribes are not listed, here. In future books, more names will be added as they are uncovered.

Cherokees

A	Berlone	Buckner	Chukelaste
Adair	Berry	Buddington	Clagget
Adams	Bird	Buford	Clark
Alberty	Birdson	Burgess	Clay
Aldrich	Black	Burney	Clifton
Allen	Blackhawk	Bursby	Clinch
Alrid	Blackwell	Burton	Coast
Alwell	Blair	Butler	Coker
Anderson	Blunt	Byrd	Colbert
Armstrong	Blythe	**C**	Coleman
Arnsby	Bolin	Caesar	Collins
Austin	Boone	Caldwell	Coody
B	Boudinot	Calvin	Cooper
Baker	Bowles	Campbell	Cordrey
Baldridge	Bowlin	Canard	Cornish
Ballard	Boyd	Carbin	Cotton
Barden	Bradford	Carr	Cox
Barker	Brady	Carson	Crapo
Barlow	Brannon	Carter	Cravens
Barnes	Braves	Cates	Crawford
Beam	Break-bill	Chambers	Crippen
Bean	Brewer	Charles	Crittendon
Beck	Brown	Chase	Crockett
Beeson	Bruce	Chatman	Crossland
Bell	Bruner	Childres	Crossley
Benge	Bryant	Choate	Cruthfield
Bentone	Buckler	Chouteau	Curls

Tribal Surnames

Curtis	Funkhauser	Holt	Lephew
D	Funter	Homes	Lett
Dalton	**G**	Hopkins	Lewis
Daniels	Ganies	Howell	Lilpe
Dansby	Garlington	Hudson	Linsey
Davis	Garnett	Huff	Litt
Dawn	Garrett	Hughes	Little
Day	Gaskins	Humphreys	Logan
Dean	Gentry	Humphry	Lorens
Deaton	Gibson	Humpries	Love
Deckman	Gilds	Hunter	Lovely
Delswood	Givens	Huston	Lowe
Dennis	Glass	**I**	Lowery
Derrick	Goff	Ireland	Luckey
Dickson	Goldsby	Irons	Luther
Diges	Graves	Irven	Lynch
Dixon	Gray	Ivory	Lyons
Dotson	Grayson	**J**	**M**
Dowling	Green	Jackson	Mabry
Drew	Griffin	James	Macken
Duncan	Grimmett	Jamison	Mackey
E	Grobes	Jenkins	Mackum
Eagle	Groomer	Jimison	MaDaniel
Eastman	Grooms	Johnson	Madden
Eaton	Grye	Jones	Malven
Ebb	Gunter	**K**	Manley
Edwards	**H**	Kell	Markham
Elliott	Haddox	Kelly	Marshall
Ellis	Hailstock	Kemp	Martin
Escoe	Hale	Kernel	Martom
Evans	Hall	Keys	Mathews
F	Hamilton	Kilpatrick	Mayberry
Fields	Hanks	King	Mayes
Fleeks	Hardman	Kirby	Mayfield
Flowers	Hardrick	Kircum	Mayo
Flynn	Harlan	Kirk	McClure
Folsom	Harland	**L**	McConnel
Ford	Harlin	Laflace	McConnell
Foreman	Harper	Landrum	McCoy
Foster	Harris	Lane	McCrackin
Francis	Hayes	Lang	McCullough
Frazier	Henderson	Langston	McCurtain
Freekman	Hickey	Lasley	McDade
French	Hicks	Ledman	McDaniels
Fry	Hight	Lee	McElroy
Fulsome	Hill	Leek	McIntosh

Tribal Surnames

McLain	Patterson	Sales	**V**
McNack	Pee	Sanders	Van Zant
McNair	Penn	Sango	Vann
McQueen	Pennington	Scales	**W**
McWaters	Perry	Scarborough	Wade
Meadonw	Perryman	Schaefer	Wagoner
Meigs	Petit	Schrimsher	Walker
Melton	Pettitt	Scott	Wallace
Merrell	Pinder	Shankling	Ward
Middleton	Poorboy	Shannon	Warren
Milam	Porlar	Shepard	Washington
Miller	Porter	Sheppard	Watie
Minnus	Posell	Silk	Watkins
Minsy	Powell	Simmons	Watson
Mitchell	Price	Skates	Wear
Monday	Purtle	Slater	Weaver
Moore	**R**	Smith	Webb
Morgan	Ragsdale	Snow	Webber
Morris	Ratcliff	Spight	Welch
Muldrow	Ray	Stanton	Welcome
Mumber	Reed	Starr	West
Mundis	Reese	Stidman	Whickliff
Munson	Reeves	Stidmon	Whiggins
Musgrove	Reid	Still	White
N	Reynolds	Sumner	Whitemire
Nalls	Richardson	Sumpter	Whitmire
Nash	Rider	Sutton	Wilfe
Nave	Riley	Swan	Williams
Nelson	Roach	Swepston	Willis
Nero	Roberson	Sykes	Wilson
Nivens	Robertson	**T**	Winters
Nolen	Robinson	Taylor	Wofford
O	Rodgers	Terry	Woodall
Owens	Roe	Theodore	Woodard
P	Rogers	Thomas	Woods
Pack	Rose	Thompson	Workman
Paine	Ross	Thornton	Wright
Parker	Roster	Townsend	**Y**
Parks	Rowe	Tucker	Young
Parris	**S**	Tyner	Youngblood

Chickasaws

A
Abram
Alberson
Albert
Alexander
Alfred
Allen
Alop
Anderson
Armstrong
Augustus
Austin
B
Bachelor
Bailey
Barlow
Barr
Beasley
Bend
Bennett
Bice
Birt
Bishop
Black
Blackwater
Block
Blue
Bly
Bower
Boyd
Brashears
Brewer
Breyson
Bright
Brooks
Brown
Bruner
Buckley
Bullocks
Burden
Burney
Butler
C

Caldwell
Campbell
Carney
Carolina
Carroll
Carson
Carter
Cass
Charles
Chawano-chbbby
Cheadle
Chery
Chesnut
Chico
Chief
Childs
Chitlow
Choate
Choice
Christiqan
Clark
Clay
Cobry
Cochran
Cohee
Coker
Colb
Colbert
Cole
Colly
Combs
Conley
Conly
Cook
Cooper
Covan
Cox
Crathers
Cravans
Cravatt
Crittenden
Crockett
Croomes

Crooms
Culpepper
Cunish
Curry
D
Daly
Daniel
Daniels
Danna
Daugherty
Davidson
Davies
Denmark
Dindy
Dinwiddie
Dixon
Doleon
Doser
Douglas
Douglass
Dumkus
Duncan
Dunford
Dyer
E
Eastman
Edwards
Eights
Elliott
Eubanks
Evans
Even
Everhart
F
Factor
Falless
Farrow
Findley
Finlay
Finley
Fisher
Fitchgerl
Flacks

Flint
Ford
Foreman
Forrester
Fort
Franklin
Frazier
Fulsom
G
Gaines
Gamble
Garrett
Gas
Gasper
Gates
Gentry
Gibbs
Gibson
Giles
Gillespie
Givens
Glover
Goff
Golden
Goldsmith
Gooden
Gorden
Graham
Grant
Grayson
Green
Greenwood
Greer
Gresham
Grey
Griffin
Grimmett
Gunn
H
Hall
Hamilton
Hampton
Harlan

Tribal Surnames

Harper	**L**	Murry	Reed
Harris	Lamey	Myers	Reese
Harry	Lawrence	**N**	Reynolds
Hawkins	Leader	Nance	Richardson
Heard	Lee	Neel	Ridge
Henderson	Lewis	Nero	Rivers
Hendersy	Ligon	Newberry	Roberts
Hennesy	Lin	Nims	Roby
Hervey	Lincoln	Nolitubby	Rodville
Hines	Lofton	North	Rollen
Hodges	Loftus	Nowell	Rose
Holder	Love	**O**	Ross
Homedy	Lynch	Ogles	Roy
Hooks	**M**	Oldhom	Russell
Horn	Mahardy	Oscar	**S**
Hornbeak	Manning	Owens	Sampson
Houser	Martin	**P**	Samuels
Houston	Mason	Paris	Scannon
HumbyNoel	Mays	Parks	Scott
Humdy	McCain	Patrick	Sealy
Humphreys	McClendon	Patton	Sears
Huntley	McClish	Paul	Shatubby
I	McCooy	Payne	Shaw
Ingram	McDermott	Peaersey	Shell
Irvins	McDonal	Pendleton	Shirley
J	McGee	Peoples	Shoeape
Jackson	McGilbray	Perry	Smallwood
Jacobs	McKenzie	Peters	Smith
Jameson	McKinney	Pettus	Sparks
Johns	McMillan	Petty	Speer
Johnson	Merriman	Phillips	Speers
Jonas	Mike	Pickens	Spencer
Jordon	Miles	Piggett	Spigener
Joseph	Miller	Plumemr	Stanfield
K	Mimmus	Poe	Stephen
Keel	Mintfield	Pollen	Stevenson
Keep	Mitchell	Porter	Stevison
Kelly	Moddy	Powell	Stewart
Kemp	Mohuntubby	Powers	Stroud
Kennedy	Molton	Preuilt	Sumers
Kersey	Monroe	Price	Summers
Kiah	Montgomery	Prince	Sutton
Kimbale	Moore	**Q**	Swindle
Kingsberry	Morrow	Quinn	**T**
Kinrick	Moses	**R**	Taylor
Kirk	Murray	Randolph	Tecumseh

Tribal Surnames

Thomas	Underwood	Watson	Wilkinson
Thompson	**V**	Watts	Willaimson
Tipkins	Van	Wesley	Willis
Tobler	Vanley	Whaley	Wilson
Toles	Vaughn	Wheeler	Windom
Townsend	Vincent	Whitaker	Wolf
Townsley	Vollen	White	Woods
Towser	**W**	Whitson	Worley
Triplett	Wade	Wilder	Wright
Tutter	Walker	Wiley	**Y**
Twyman	Walton	Wiliams	Yates
Tyner	Ward	Wilkerson	Yocubby
Tyson	Washington	Wilkes	Young
U	Waters	Wilkins	Younger

Choctaws

A
Abbott
Abram
Adams
Adamson
Ainsworth
Alberson
Alexander
Allen
Anderson
Arnold
Askew
Austin
B
Bagley
Bailey
Banks
Barber
Bardner
Barley
Barr
Barrett
Barrows
Bary
Bassett
Battie
Battiece
Battiest
Beams
Bearden
Beavers
Beckwith
Beeson
Belcher
Bell
Belvin
Benson
Bibbs
Bidden
Biggs

Binks
Bird
Birdsong
Blackwater
Blair
Bledsoe
Blocker
Blue
Blunt
Boatwright
Boldin
Bolding
Bonham
Bordon
Bowers
Boyd
Boyles
Brack
Bradley
Brady
Brasco
Brashears
Brewer
Briggs
Briley
Brown
Bruce
Brumley
Bruner
Bryant
Buckman
Buckner
Buffington
Bulger
Burks
Burris
Burton
Busby
Butler
Byrd

C
Caephus
Cahill
Cain
Campbell
Carney
Carr
Carroll
Carson
Carter
Caruthers
Cass
Cennis
Chalk
Chambers
Chandler
Chapman
Charry
Chatman
Cheadle
Chester
Chilton
Chism
Choate
Christian
Clark
Clay
Clayton
Cleveland
Cochran
Cohee
Cohes
Colbert
Cole
Coleman
Colly
Conard
Cook
Cotton
Cox

Craig
Cravens
Crawford
Cris
Crittendon
Crooms
Croons
Crutchfield
Cubit
Culver
Cunford
D
Dana
Dangerfield
Daniels
Daugherty
Davis
Demps
Demus
Dizer
Dockins
Dodd
Dodson
Donegay
Douglas
Douglass
Duckett
Dumas
Duncan
Durant
E
Eastman
Easton
Edd
Edwards
Eights
Ellis
Ellison
Elridge
Epps

Tribal Surnames

Ervin
Eubanks
Evans
Everidge
Evrett
Ewing
Ewings
F
Factory
Farris
Featherspoon
Featherston
Ferguson
Fields
Finley
Fisher
Flack
Fleeks
Flint
Floyd
Folsom
Foreman
Franklin
Frazier
Freeman
Freeney
Freeny
French
Fullbright
Fulsom
G
Gables
Gaffney
Galbert
Galloway
Gant
Garland
Gay
Gibson
Gidden
Givens
Glover
Gooding
Goodlow
Graham
Graham

Graves
Gray
Grayson
Green
Greenwood
Greer
Gross
Grundy
Guess
Guest
H
Haley
Halford
Hall
Hampton
Hardlan
Harkins
Harnage
Harris
Harrison
Harvey
Hatley
Hawkins
Haywood
Henderson
Henry
Hester
Hicks
Hill
Hilliard
Hills
Hines
Hodges
Hogan
Holford
Hollaway
Hollin
Holt
Homer
Hoppy
Horn
Hornback
Horton
Hotchkins
Hotchkiss
Howell

Hughes
Humdy
Humes
Humphrey
Hunter
Hutchins
Hutchison
Hyatt
I
Ingram
Irving
J
Jackson
Jacob
Jamerson
James
Jeater
Jeffers
Jefferson
Jeffries
Jeter
John
Johnson
Johnston
Jolly
Jones
Jordon
Joseph
Judy
Justice
K
Keel
Keith
Kemp
Kendrick
Kendricks
Kincade
King
Kingsbury
Kirk
L
Larkin
Last
Lathers
Lawrence
Lawson

Lee
Leflore
LeFlore
Leftridge
Lenox
Leppord
Lewis
Liggins
Lison
Littlejohn
Livingsyton
Logan
Looney
Love
Lovelace
Low
Lowery
Lownen
Lynch
M
Mabry
Mackey
Mackey
Mahardy
Mann
Manning
Mansfield
Mat-ub-bee
Maturby
Maupin
Maxwell
May
Mayes
Mays
Maytubbe
Maytuby
McAfee
McCarty
McChristian
McClendon
McCloud
McCoy
McCurtain
McDaniel
McDonald
McGee

Tribal Surnames

McGilbry	**O**	Rentie	Stakohaka
McGuire	Oats	Reynolds	Stanley
McKee	Oliver	Rice	Star
McKinley	Osborn	Richards	Starly
McKinney	Oscar	Riddle	Starr
McNeill	Overton	Ridge	Stephenson
McQuilla	Owens	Riffington	Stevenson
Meadows	Owles	Riley	Stewart
Meggs	**P**	Riston	Striblin
Meighbors	Paris	Roberts	Stribling
Merritts	Parish	Robinson	Stubblefield
Miles	Parker	Roby	Suton
Miller	Parkins	Roebuck	Sutton
Mills	Partilla	Rogers	**T**
Milton	Patterson	Rose	Taylor
Minner	Patton	Ross	Teel
Mitchell	Payton	Russell	Thomas
Moore	Pearson	**S**	Thompson
Moors	Pendleton	Sakki	Thurman
Morgan	Perry	Sams	Timpson
Morotn	Phelps	Samuels	Tinkshell
Moses	Phillips	Sandridge	Tis
Mosley	Pickens	Scott	Titus
Moss	Pierce	Seely	Triplett
Munn	Pitchlynn	Sell	Tucker
Murchison	Pitner	Severe	Turner
Murphy	Poleon	Sexton	Tyler
Murray	Powell	Shaw	Tyner
Musgrove	Pratt	Shelby	Tyson
N	Price	Shelton	**V**
Nail	Prince	Shephard	Valliant
Nash	Pryor	Shield	Vaughn
Neal	Pulcher	Shields	Vinson
Neioll	Purdy	Shirley	Virgil
Nelson	Pursley	Shoals	Voryd
Newberry	**R**	Sholes	**W**
Newton	Radford	Short	Wade
Nolan	Railback	Sifax	Wagoner
Noland	Read	Simmons	Waldron
Nolen	Rechardson	Simpson	Walford
Norman	Record	Sims	Walker
Norris	Rector	Sindham	Walls
Nourvle	Reddick	Smallwood	Walter
Nunley	Reed	Smith	Walton
Nunnally	Reeder	Spencer	Walzer
Nunnely	Reeves	Spring	Ward

Ware
Warner
Warren
Warrior
Washington
Waters
Watson
Webb
Welch
West
Whitaker
Whitby
White
Wilburn
Wilkins
Williams
Willis
Wilson
Wimbley
Wine
Woods
Wooter
Worthen
Wright
Y
Yocubby
Young

Creeks

A	Blackstone	Childs	Davis
Abrams	Boone	Choteau	Davison
Adams	Bowleg	Clark	Dean
Add	Bowlegs	Clayton	Deleny
Adkins	Bowman	Clinton	Deloney
Alberty	Boyd	Coats	Dennis
Alec	Bradberry	Cobb	Derisaw
Aleck	Bradford	Cobbrey	Dindy
Alex	Brady	Cohee	Dixon
Alexander	Brewster	Colbert	Doil
Allen	Brinkley	Cole	Dolman
Andrew	Bristor	Coleman	Douglass
Andy	Broadnax	Collin	Downs
Ard	Brooks	Colling	Doyle
Asbury	Brown	Colly	Drake
Atkins	Bruner	Conner	Draper
Austin	Buckner	Connor	Drew
B	Buffington	Cooks	Duff
Bailey	Bumpus	Coon	Dunbar
Baker	Bunn	Corbray	Durant
Ballard	Burgess	Cousins	Dyle
Banks	Burnett	Cowans	**E**
Barber	Burney	Cox	Easley
Barker	Burton	Crabtree	Eastman
Barnes	Butler	Craig	Edwards
Barnett	Byrd	Crane	Epperson
Barnette	**C**	Craw	Escoe
Barrett	Caesar	Crossley	Eubanks
Bates	Canada	Crosslin	Evans
Batt	Canard	Cruel	Everett
Batts	Cannon	Cudjo	**F**
Bean	Carlina	Cudjoe	Factor
Bear	Carliner	Cuff	Faro
Beaver	Carnard	Culley	Faster
Bell	Carolina	Cully	Fee
Berry	Carr	Curns	Fester
Berryhill	Carson	Curtis	Fields
Billy	Carter	Cyrus	Fife
Birney	Chambers	**D**	Fink
Bishop	Charles	Dan	Fisher
Blackburn	Childers	Daniels	Flannagan

Flint
Flowers
Flynn
Folsom
Ford
Foreman
Forman
Foster
Fox
Frances
Francis
Franklin
Frazier
Froe
Fryday
Fulsom
G
Gains
Garmon
Garrett
Gaskine
Gates
Gaylord
Geary
Gentry
Gibson
Gilbert
Glover
Golden
Gooden
Gordan
Graham
Grant
Gray
Grayson
Green
Gregory
Greyson
Griffin
Griggs
Grimmett
Guess
Gwin
H
Hamilton
Hammonds

Hampton
Hardgray
Hardrige
Harper
Harris
Harrison
Harrod
Harvey
Hasup
Hawkins
Hayes
Haynes
Henderson
Henry
Herod
Hershey
Hickles
Higginbottom
Hill
Hills
Hobbs
Hodge
Holloway
Holmes
Homer
Hope
Horn
Houston
Howard
Hudson
Hughes
Hunley
Hutton
I
Irving
Isaac
Isaacs
Island
J
Jack
Jackson
Jacobs
James
Jameson
Jamison
Jefferson

Jimmerson
Joans
Job
Johnson
Jonas
Jones
K
Kanard
Kell
Kelley
Kelly
Kemp
Kennedy
Kernal
Kernel
Keyes
Keys
Kidd
King
Knowles
Krooms
L
Lacy
Lampkins
Landrum
Lawrence
Lee
Leffard
Lester
Lewis
Lincoln
Little
Logan
Loneon
Long
Love
Lovett
Low
Lowe
Lowery
Luckey
Lucy
Lunnon
Luster
Lyons
M

Mackey
Mahardy
Makins
Malvern
Malvery
Manac
Manuel
Marshal
Martin
Mathews
Mayberry
Mayes
Mayfield
Mayson
McClain
McDaniel
McGee
McGilbra
McGilbray
McGirt
McHenry
McIntosh
McKellop
McKinney
McNac
McNack
McSimms
McSims
Meriwether
Mike
Miles
Miller
Millett
Mimms
Minas
Minnis
Monday
Monroe
Moody
Moore
Morey
Morgan
Morris
Morrison
Mosley
Mullen

Mure	Pettitt	Robison	Solomon
Murphy	Philips	Rodgers	Sookey
Murray	Phillips	Roe	Spaks
Murrell	Pierce	Rogers	Spencer
Murrill	Pippins	Rorex	Spring
Myers	Poldo	Rose	Standford
Myles	Pompey	Ross	Stanford
N	Pond	Rowe	Starr
Nail	Ponds	Russell	Staten
Nash	Porlar	**S**	Steadham
Nave	Porter	Samuel	Stendham
Neal	Post	Samuels	Stephens
Nero	Postoak	Sancho	Stepney
Nevens	Potts	Sanders	Stevens
Nevins	Pratt	Sandy	Stewart
Newell	Price	Sango	Stidham
Newman	Primmer	Scales	Street
Nichols	Primous	Scott	Stroy
Nix	Primus	Scruggs	Sugar
Noble	Prince	Seaman	**T**
Nomman	Pyles	Sears	Tab
Norfer	**Q**	Segro	Tanner
Norwood	Quabner	Sells	Taylor
O	Quinn	Serrell	Tecumseh
Olden	**R**	Sevel	Thomas
Oldham	Ragen	Sewel	Thompson
Osborn	Ragsdale	Sewell	Thursday
Osborne	Randolph	Sharper	Tiger
Overton	Rector	Shaw	Tipton
Owen	Redmon	Shawnee	Tittle
Owens	Redmond	Shelton	Tobey
P	Redmouth	Shepard	Tobler
Parker	Reed	Sherman	Toliver
Parlor	Rentie	Shields	Tolliver
Paro	Rice	Shoals	Tom
Patrick	Richard	Shoto	Toney
Patterson	Richards	Siah	Trotter
Payne	Riley	Sier	Tucker
Pea	Roane	Simmons	Turner
Perkins	Robbins	Simon	Typer
Perry	Roberson	Sims	**V**
Perryman	Roberts	Skeeter	Vann
Peter	Robertson	Smith	Vannoy
Peters	Robins	Sneed	Vaughn
Peterson	Robinson	Snowden	Verner

Vincent
Virgel
W
Wade
Walcot
Walden
Walker
Wallace
Wallas
Walton
Wamble
Ware
Warner
Warrior
Washington
Watson
Webber
Webster
Welch
Welsh
Wheat
White
Williams
Willis
Wilson
Wisner
Wofford
Wollard
Woodall
Woodard
Woodley
Woods
Wright
Y
Young

Seminoles

A
Aaron
Abb
Abey
Abraham
Adam
Adams
Ahaisse
A-ha-la-ko-chee
Ahaloke
Ah-ho-he
Ah-weep-ka
Albert
Alberty
Alec
Aleck
Alecky
Alex
Alexander
Alfa
Alfred
Alice
Alicky
Allen
Alley
Allie
Amesta
Amey
Amos
Amy
Anderson
Anna
Annie
Annoche
Archibald
Archockee
Archole
B
Baby
Baker
Barkus
Barnett
Barney
Barricklow
Bean
Bear
Beard
Becky
Bemo
Bennett
Berry
Betsy
Bettie
Billy
Bottley
Bowlegs
Brown
Bruce
Bruner
Bryant
Buck
Buddy
Bull
Burden
Burgess
Butler
C
Caesar
Canard
Carbechochee
Carbiticher
Carolina
Carpitche
Carr
Carter
Catcher
Catchoche
Charlesey
Charley
Charlie
Charty
Checotah
Che-da-ka
Cheeska
Chepaney
Cheparney
Cheponoska
Chippee
Chisholm
Chochee
Choharjo
Chosey
Chotka
Chotke
Chotkey
Choya
Chulma
Chumsey
Chupco
Chupcogee
Church
Cindy
Clark
Cloud
Cobb
Co-e-see
Coffee
Coker
Coley
Concharty
Condella
Condulle
Conhecha
Conner
Co-nok-kee
Contaley
Coody
Cooper
Cornelius
Cosar
Cotcha
Cowake
Co-wok-o-chee
Cox
Crain
Crane
Crow
Cudjo
Cudjoe
Cully
Cumpsey
Cumseh
Cundy
Cunny
Cunsah
Cynda
Cyrus
D
Daily
Dandy
Daniel
Davey
David
Davis
Davison
Dean
Deer
Dennis
Dicey
Dillsa
Dinah
Dindy
Dosar
Doser
Doyle
Drew
Dunford
Dunlap
Dyal
Dyer
E
Echoille
Edmond
Eliza
Elizabeth
Ellen

The Black American Handbook for Survival

Elochee	Ground	Jacksy	Kinnona
Elsa	**H**	Jacob	Kissie
Elsie	Hagie	Jakey	Kith-lee
Emartha	Haney	James	Kotska
Emarthla	Hanna	Janey	**L**
Emarthoge	Hannah	Jannati	Lanego
Emmy	Hardy	Jefferson	Larney
Emoche	Harjo	Jemima	Lasley
En-le-te-ke	Harjoche	Jennetta	Leader
Es-ho-po-na-ka	Harrison	Jennie	Leah
Estachukseho-ke	Hatty	Jesse	Lelusse
	Hawkins	Jimmey	Lena
Estomethla	Hayecha	Jimmie	Letka
Eunasse	Hayes	Jimmy	Lewis
F	Henne-ho-chee	Jimpka	Liley
Factor		Jimpsey	Lina
Fanny	Henny	Joanna	Lincoln
Fay	Henry	Jo-co-chee	Lindsey
Fekhoniye	Hepsey	Joe	Litka
Fife	Hesahoka	John	Little
Fik-hith-ka	Hill	Johnie	Lizzie
Fish	Hilly	Johnoche	Lodie
Fixico	Hochifke	Johnsey	London
Flanley	Hoktochee	Johnson	Lopka
Foster	Hoktoke	Jonah	Losata
Fox	Holata	Jonasse	Lottie
Freeman	Holatka	Jones	Lotty
Fulsom	Hollins	Joney	Louie
Fuswa	Holmes	Joseph	Louisa
Futcha-hoke	Hopoille	Josey	Lousanna
Futopeche	Hotulke	Joshua	Lovett
G	Hulbutta	Judy	Lowe
Gaines	Hulhoke	July	Lowery
Gano	Hulleah	Jumper	Lowesa
George	Hully	June	Lowine
Gibbs	Hulwa	**K**	Lowiney
Gibson	Hutche	Kamabe	Lozana
Gibsy	Hutke	Kane	Lucina
Goat	**I**	Kaney	Lucy
Gooden	Ida	Katie	Lula
Gordon	Iley	Katy	Lumba
Grant	Ishmael	Kenah	Lumsey
Gray	Island	Keno	Lundo
Grayson	**J**	Ke-pa-ya	Lusoche
Greenleaf	Jacksey	Key	Lustey
	Jackson	King	**M**

Through the 21st Century – Vol. I

Mahale	Minda	Nicey	Pon-no-kee
Mahardy	Mingo	Nitchey	Porter
Malinda	Misselda	Nitey	Possuk
Mandy	Missena	Noah	Pottey
Maney	Missey	Noble	Powell
Manuel	Missie	Nokoseka	Proctor
Marcus	Mitchell	Nokusile	Pullotka
Marcy	Mitchile	Nora	Puncho
Maria	Mogee	Noska	Punka
Marks	Mokoyike	Nuksokoche	Punluste
Marpiyecher	Moleya	**O**	Putkeh
Marshal	Mollie	Okfuska	**R**
Marshall	Molly	Okfuskey	Rabbit
Martha	Monacheke	Okfusky	Raiford
Marthla	Monday	Omayaye	Reed
Martin	Monkah	Osborne	Renton
Marty	Mooney	Otheche	Renty
Mary	Moore	**P**	Rhoda
Matuth-hoke	Moppin	Palmer	Riley
Maude	Morgan	Paney	Ripley
McCoy	Morris	Parney	Robert
McCulla	Morrison	Parnoche	Roberts
McGeisey	Mosar	Parnosa	Roe
McGeisy	Moses	Par-nos-co-che	Rosanna
McGirt	Mot-hoh-ye		Ross
McIntosh	Mulcussey	Parnoskey	**S**
McNac	Mulcy	Paroah	Sa-che-meche
Mecco	Mulgusse	Parsosee	
Meley	Mulleah	Passake	Saketheche
Melishkoche	Mundy	Pa-ta-ge	Sakoeka
Melisse	Mungo	Payne	Sakteke
Melo	Munnah	Pennose	Saley
Meney	Muthoye	Perryman	Salina
Mesale	**N**	Peter	Salinda
Mesaley	Nancy	Phena	Sallie
Metetakee	Nannie	Phenie	Sally
Micco	Napoeche	Pheobe	Salma
Miley	Narcome	Philip	Saloche
Miller	Natukse	Phillip	Sam
Milley	Nellie	Phillips	Samby
Millie	Nellsie	Pilot	Samele
Mills	Nelly	Pochuswa	Sammah
Milly	Nelsey	Polly	Sammy
Milsey	Ne-ma	Pompey	Samochee
Mimey	Nero	Ponkilla	Sampson
Mina	Nevins	Ponluste	Samuel

The Black American Handbook for Survival

Sancho	Stafey	Tolomka	Wise
Sando	Stanton	Tommy	Wisey
Sandrige	Steel	Toney	Wisner
Sandy	Stephenson	Tulla	Witlow
Sango	Stepney	Tulsay	Wolf
Sapalpake	Steppe	Turner	Wood
Sapehunka	Stewart	**U**	Wotko
Sapokhohthe	Stidham	Ut-tley	Wright
Sarber	Street	**V**	Wyetka
Sarney	Suc-car-see	Vann	**Y**
Scipio	Sullivan	**W**	Ya-fo-la-gee
Scott	Sumka	Wadsworth	Yahola
Seeley	Sumpsey	Waitey	Yakopuche
Sefah	Sunday	Wakkie	Yamie
Seharney	Sunny	Walker	Yanah
Sehoka	Susanna	Wallace	Yarber
Sehunka	Susey	Walter	Yarnah
Selba	Susie	War-le-do	Yekcha
Selda	Suthoye	Warrior	Yoney
Selma	Su-wa-key	Washington	Youngs
Semissee	**T**	Wasutke	Yowe
Semleteke	Tahike	Watson	
Sena	Talmascy	Watty	
Se-ne	Talmasey	Weattie	
Sentevey	Tanyan	Webster	
Sigler	Tar-co-sar	Weely	
Silla	Tayeche	Wellington	
Silla	Taylor	Wells	
Sillah	Tecumseh	Wesley	
Sim-e-di-ha-kee	Teller	West	
Simena	Tena	Wetley	
Simma	Te-tah-ke	White	
Sim-me-te-da-kee	Tewe	Whitfield	
	Tewee	Wildcat	
	Thahoyane	Willea	
Simon	Thasate	William	
Sissie	Thlocco	Williamkee	
Sissy	Thocco	Williams	
Skiff	Thomas	Williamse	
Smith	Thompson	Williamsee	
Solomon	Tiger	Willie	
Sona	Tikahche	Willis	
Sonny	Ti u na	Wilsey	
Sowanoke	Tobie	Wilson	
Sowatske	Toche	Winey	
Spencer	Tolmochusse	Winton	

Through the 21st Century – Vol. I

SELECTED BIBLIOGRAPHIES

The books listed here are a start for all people interested in discovering there true Ancestral roots. Please note how the label of Indians becomes Negro, these terms are interchanged often to speak about the same people.

As you read some of these books, you will find conflicting information about their stories. You will also find the older the book, the more accurate the information.

Please Note:
The information you will find is very painful and you may feel very angry over what has happened to "our" Ancestors and what is currently happening to you and your life. Please do not hate. Hate is not the answer. Remember our Ancestors were chosen by God to be "the Keepers" of this great land. Take a break, fill out your petitions, write a book, find new areas that need to be researched, and make a positive change for life and for our future generations.
** REPRESENTS BOOK RATING

It time to Heal,

this is a new day ...

this will be a new dawn.

★★★ "Letters & Notes On The North American Indians" George Catlin, Edited by Michael M. Mooney, Clarkson N. Potter, Inc/ Crown Pub. (1975)

★★★★ "History de la Florida" by Garcilaso de la Vega's

Selected Bibliographies/Index

- ★★★ "Chickasaw Nation" by James Malone, John Morton pub.(1922)
- ★★★★ 1796-1872: "Letters & Notes On The North American Indians" George Catlin; Original work published in 1841 under the title "Letters and Notes on the Manners, Customs, and Conditions of the North American Indians" *(A very good book for physical descriptions, before the invasion of the Europeans)*
- ★★★ "The Mound Builders" by R. Silverberg, Published by Athens, Ohio University Press, 1986
- ★★★★ "Indian Slavery in Colonel Times; Studies in History, Economics and Public Law" by Almos Wheeler, Corner House pub.(1970), printed in 1913

  "Holy Bible" King James version - New Testament
- ** "Our Nation Archives" - Erick Bruun & Jay Crosby
- ** "First Americans" - Time Life Books, 1993
- ** "Metaphysical Bible Dictionary"
- ★★★ "Hidden Cities: The Discovery and Loss of Ancient North American Civilization" by Roger G. Kennedy, New York, The Free Press 1994
- ★★★ "Black Spark, White Fire" by Richard Poe, Prima Publishing
- ★★ "The Paradigm Conspiracy - How our Systems of Government, Church, School and Culture, Violate our Human Potential", by Brenton Largest / Denise Brenton, Hazeldon Pub (1996)
- ★★ "Lost Tribes and Promised Lands"
  by Rondalds Sanders

The Black American Handbook for Survival

★★★ "America's Secret Destiny" by Robery Heironimus, P.D. Destiny Books pub.(1989)

★★★ "The Only Land They Ever Knew - The Tragic Story of the Southern Indians" by James Leitch

The (8th grade) Georgia Studies book: "Our State and the Nation" by Carl Vinson Institute of Government, The University of Georgia

★★ "Indian America" by Gurko

"Black Indians" by William Katz

"Cherokees In Pre-Columbian Times, 1825-1910" by Cyrus Thomas

"The Constitution of the United States" by Weber

"Fulcrums Of Change" by Jan R. Carew, 1988

The U.S. Department of Interior

Due to the intense international web search needed to complete this book, I will not be able to list all the web sites researched. Many of the sites for information are now closed to the public. However, I will recommend that you search for the following sites: *Missouri Institute on Amerindian Studies* or *Hutchison Institute.*

- Have Fun!!!

Index of Questions

Index of Questions
Chapter 1- The Hidden Racial Identity

How many races are there?
What geographical areas do the races of people live?
Why do all people have a homeland and birthright given to them by God?
What races do Black Americans represent?
What section of the world do the Indian race inhabit?
What does the term Indian mean?
How many groups of indigenous people lived in North America before discovery?
Which group had the largest territory and population in North America?
Which group is today's Black Americans?
Who are the Mound Builders?
How many years did the Mound builders live here?
What is a Matriarchal civilization?
What do the people who are called the Mound Builders of North to Southeastern America look like?
What kind of hair do the real Indigenous North American people have?
What about the eyes?
What about skin color?
What is the physical stature of the Mound Builders of North America ?
Are there many skin color ranges for American Indians Called Mound Builders?
Do American Indians of North & South Eastern Nations of Mound builders have straight, black hair, and tan or white skin?
Are West Africans and American Indians the same people?
If Indian people are termed Black and African people are termed Black. What is the real identity of today's Black

American people, and how did the Europeans tell the difference?
How can a Dark-skinned person living in America as a descendant of a Negro know his roots?
What happened to the Nations of Mound Builder's people to make them Vanish in the 1700's?
What happened after all the Indians became Negroes in the 1700-1800's?
Are the people called Cherokee or north and Southeastern Indians today the real American Indians?
Who are classified as Native Americans today?
What does the term " Native American " mean?
Who are the Nations of North & South Eastern Black American Mound Builders?
Why aren't Black Americans also considered Native Americans?
. Why can most Black Americans today identify with an ancestral Indian grandparent?
Why didn't my grandparents tell me the whole story?
Why are my ancestors Indian and I are not?
Why do Black American people today dismiss their Indian ancestral identity?
Why do ALL Black Americans belong in America? Pg30

Chapter 2- Hidden / Vanished Civilization

What was Our Ancestral name?
What does the word Choctaw mean ?
Where did our Ancestral civilization of people come from?
Who are the people who came from the Bearing straits?
What is the name of the North American continent?
What kind of civilization existed in North America?
What kind of Society did we have?
What is a Matriarchal Society?

The Black American Handbook for Survival

What is a Matriarchal conscious of the " principles of feminism?
What is the meaning of the word America?
What was the name of our Empire/Nation?
What kind of government did we have?
What is the name of our government?
How big was the original Mound builders civilization of Black American people?
Today what states are divided into this land?
How many people lived during the Black American civilization at time of European discovery?
How many communities or tribes were here at time of discovery by Desoto?
What was our ancestral form of transportation?
How large was the trade network of our ancestors?
What was the character of the indigenous Black American man?
What was the character of the Black American woman?
What about the Moral character of "Our" Indigenous Black American Ancestors?
What kind of religion did Our Ancestors have?
Did our ancestors have a written language?
Did our ancestors have libraries?
What was our main technology?
What foods did we cultivate?
What was our Black American diet for thousands of years?
What kind of clothes did we wear?
What were the indigenous Black Americans Mound Builder's favorite activities?
Did the Black American Mound builder's ancestors have big families?
How big was the average family?
What was considered a Rich family by the Black American Ancestors?
What kind of education did the children receive?
Did we live in tepee's

How long was the life span of the Black American ancestors?
Did our Ancestors develop their own medicine?
Did we have the diseases we have today?
What diseases did the Europeans Invaders bring?
What animals are not indigenous to this land?
What foods did the European bring?
What happened to our civilizations economy and powerful trade network?
Did our Ancestors realize the agenda of the European people who was invading our shores.?
Why don't Black Americans have a united trade network today?

Chapter 3- The Hidden Ancestral Identity of today's Black American

* Who are the indigenous Anasazi people in the Old Testament in the bible?
* Are Black Americans or Anasazi Nations of Mound builders the people who were given, as promised by God, a new homeland in the Old testament in the Bible?
* What happened to the people who lived in North Africa who chose to live self centered and consumes nature?
* What happened after Ramsey declared himself a God over Kemmit or Egypt?
* What is patriarchal consciousness?
* What is a Patriarchal society?
* How did the Patriarchal overcome the Matriarchal way of living?
* What happened to Kemmit or Egypt after the raping, killing and enslavement of the women by men?
* What is the name of the people who are the remaining descendants of the Egyptians of North Africa?
* Who are the Muirs?
* What does the word "Slave" mean?

The Black American Handbook for Survival

- * Are the Muirs and the Black American /Anasazi Mound builders called Indians the same people?
- * What do Nubian, Atlantis, Egyptians, Hebrews, Omecs, Aztecs, Mayans, Mound builder, Indians, Negro's, Mulattoes, colored, Afro-Americans, and today's Black Americans have in common?
- * Do the North African Muirs have claim to the Ancestral Homeland as Indigenous Black Americans?
- * How did the European people regain control of their heritage from the Muirs?

Chapter 4- It started with Columbus:

- * Who authorized Columbus military voyage?
- * What was the purpose for the expeditions to find new lands for Columbus
- * Why did Columbus choose to sail across the sea?
- * What kind of society did the Spanish need to find in order to conquer them?
- * Why is it important to the European predators to seek out races of people who are operating in an unconscious state of wholeness with the planet?
- * What would the Europeans have to do in order to break the protection, the races of the planet had from living within natural law?
- * Did Columbus discover North America?
- * Why is Columbus given credit for finding the America's?
- * What did this land look like at the time of Spanish Moor discovery?
- * What happened after Columbus discovered the New World?
- * When was mainland of North America discovered?
- * What did the Spanish do to implement Patriarchal religion of Christianity into the American people?

* What is the difference between Patriarchal religion and Matriarchal religion

Chapter 5- UNDERSTANDING SLAVERY- THE CREATION OF THE NEGRO

* What is the purpose of capturing and using people for mechanical labor?
* How many races have experience being robbed or enslaved during their history?
* When did slavery start?
* Who would have to be enslaved for the knowledge to produce from the environment in America?
* How long did European slavery thrive in West Africa?
* Where were the West African people transported?
* When did slavery start in North America?
* Were Africans brought over to America, in the 1500's?
* What is the percentage of Africans who came as slaves to North America?
* Why didn't Europeans bring Africans over to North America?
* Where were the Africans and Indians taken to?
* Where did African and Indians mix?
* What European countries participated in the slave trade of the North and South American Anasazi people called Indians?
* How was the first economic trade started for Europeans in North America?
* Do Black Americans have West African ancestry?
* What was the average life span of a person once captured in the 1500's-1700?
* How did the European conquer " Our" Indigenous ancestors?
* How did the Europeans capture large numbers of people?
* What is the profile of a slave?

The Black American Handbook for Survival

- How long did the exportation of " Our" indigenous Black American ancestors exist as slaves?
- What was different about the English agenda for slavery?
- How did the European colonist apply their agenda through slavery?
- How did the acquisition of children for the slave trade in Anasazi people termed- Indians work between colonies?
- What does branding mean?
- What has to be done to the person to make them release their personal power?
- What is rape?
- Why was it necessary to rape the children?
- What happened as a result from enslaving generations of Anasazi youth?
- What is a Nigger?
- What did the European colonist do after the children were broken into slavery to maintain there emotional bondage?
- What does the term Negro mean?
- What is the definition of a "Negro as a slave?
- Did Anasazi women (black American) have babies by their captors?
- How did the European infiltrate our Ancestral Anasazi Bloodline?
- Are today's Black American mixed with White Blood?
- Why does today's Black American have white sir names?
- Are all Black Americans descendants of imported Slaves or Negro's?
- Why did many Black Americans choose to accept living as Negro's?

Through the 21st Century – Vol. I

Chapter 6- United States vs. Black America

* Where did the African story " The Middle Passage" come from?
* Why are Black Americans educated to look towards Africa for their identity?
* Why wasn't I taught about my Indian ancestors and their experience as slaves in school?
* How do the European educational system maintain a slave mentality among today's Black American?
* Are today's Black Americans citizens of the United States?
* What does " Privilege to " mean?
* What did the indigenous Americans unknowingly release for the recognition of the privilege of being a public citizen?
* When did I sign my rights away?
* Why must racism exist in America?
* What is " genocide"?
* How is this agenda effectively implemented ?

Chapter 7- Spiritual Understanding of the Black American Holocaust.

- What are the spiritual lesson to be learned from this holocaust of our People?
- What did the European man offer the Black American man that put the people and future generations into bondage?
- What lessons do Anasazi/Black American women have to learn?
- What do Anasazi/ Black American people have to do to heal themselves?
- Is money the answer?.

The Black American Handbook for Survival

Selected Bibliographies/Index

Symbol Of the Hidden Heritage 178

The Black American Hidden Heritage logo

This logo, as a whole, represents the new symbol of the Legacy of the Ancestral Heritage of Today's Black American People.

"The Ancient Ones"

Incorporated within this symbol:

The **ankh** is a symbol used by The Ancient Ones to represent life and its opposing energies, as a cycle for regeneration.

The **feather** is symbolic of the Spirit of The Ancient Ones, representing the force that creates the movement through which the opposing energies cycle and generate life. The Spirit is thought of as moving with the wind and the bird is the only creation that soars WITH the Spirit and literally dances with God.

The **ancient pyramid** was once called a fire temple because our Ancestors believed that life began with a spark of fire.

The **ankh**, the **feather**, and the **pyramid** are touching each other in a line - the way our Ancestors' heritage is told: holding the story, in spirit, in stone, and in wisdom for the memory and elevation of our PEOPLE.

Eleyé Eifé has been a professional artist and illustrator for 10 years. She currently prefers to work in charcoal and acrylic paints. She believes that her artistic inspiration comes from her ancestors. She was told, in prophecy, that she and her daughter would be used by the Spirit to reveal to the people an Ancient art form. It has always been her desire to be a vehicle for the expression of the Ancestral Spirit and to teach that unfolding knowledge through her visual talents. **THE TIME HAS COME.**

✴

*Indians, Negroes,
and today's
Black Americans
Descendants of the Anasazi Nations of North
American Mound builders
have NOT been abandoned
by the Holy Spirit…*

they are NOT losers!

*When United with the Holy ancestral Sprit
Manifest
the Greatest Healing Power
on Earth!*

✴

Quantum Leap Spiritual Life Center

What is Quantum Leap Spiritual Life Center?
Quantum Leap Spiritual Life Center is an interfaith, organization that provides information and instruction to Black Americans regarding their Ancestral spiritual understanding of Natural Law, true identity, heritage and culture as **the indigenous people of the America's and Caribbean.**

Our motto:
HOW CAN WE SERVE?
Healing people, family bloodlines, communities and ultimately our Heritage.

The mission of Quantum Leap S.L.C. is to aid Black American people in returning to their inherited path from their ancestors who are the planet keepers called " the Anasazi people". So they once again can

**LOVE WITHOUT JUDGEMENT,
ACT WITHOUT Prejudice
AND
HONOR WITHOUT NEED.**

We support and encourage the embracing of the ancestral life concepts that maintain the foundation of our people, our families emotional balance, mental well-being and unity.
We teach people to embrace life challenges using natural law as a defense against all opposition we may face. All people can overcome any form of mental and emotional bondage that has been inflicted on them using the Natural law given to us from God.

Center Services
- **Spiritual Perspective**, a monthly newsletter and a personal advice service

The Black American Handbook for Survival

- **The School of Ancient Wisdom & Healing Arts** – offers instruction and certification programs in ministry and holistic healing.
  Sacred Ancestral Journey's Retreats- Embracing Ancestral heritage and healing of the heart.
  Quantum Leap SLC publications- dedicated to revealing the Hidden story of the Indigenous American holocaust.

On line store and catalog .featuring- ancestral Heritage products for the spirit..

For in-depth and detailed understanding of Black American heritage and history. Rev.RaDine offers lecture series." The Hidden Identity & Heritage of the American Negro" For an in dept understanding and application of Natural Law. Rev.. RaDine Amen-ra has a lecture series " Seminars for Soulful Living"

If you would like to receive a catalog of products and information about future workshops, lectures, retreats, courses and events sponsored by Quantum Leap S.L.C.

Contact. Quantum Leap S.L.C. 1-877-571-9788 or go our web page at Quantumleapslc.org or blackamericanhandbook.com

About the Author

"There are few instances in our lives when we meet a person who is truly Divine. Rev. RaDine Amen-ra is one such person"
Antonio Green-Rolling out magazine

Rev. RaDine Amen-ra is an Indigenous born American, from the Heritage linage of a Chickasaw mother and Cherokee/Yamesse father. Rev. RaDine N.D. L.M.T. L.C.T.is an ordained Interfaith Minister with over 20 years experience in Psychotherapy, Human resource development, and Holistic Health. Rev. RaDine is a Healer, researcher, lecturer and founder of Quantum Leap Spiritual Life Center located in Atlanta Georgia. The mission of the center is to assist the Black American people to recognize their indigenous birth-right identity, heal from the bondage of slavery, and the rape of their true ancestral identity, heritage, culture, and homeland. .

Rev. RaDine Amen-ra was asked by many to teach her wonderful awareness of life and soul understanding. As a survivor of a near death tragedy herself Rev. RaDine was lead to uncover the larger more profound understanding about life. Surrendering her life to her spiritual soul, and following Natural law.-she in return received gifts beyond her wildest dreams and expectations. The most profound gift was the revealing and validation of her true ancestral identity and the Ancestral identity of 50 million or more people who live under the classification of Afro- Americans. This profound Grace alone has made it clear to her why her life and all the Negro People of America is SO IMPORTANT to HUMMANITY. She joyfully accepts the purpose of her life for the healing of her people, which will allow the healing of all the people on the planet

The Black American Handbook for Survival

It is Time……. It is Time…. Time has come……… for your light……..
Look towards the sun the children of Amerriqui…………
For this dawn will bring a new day……...

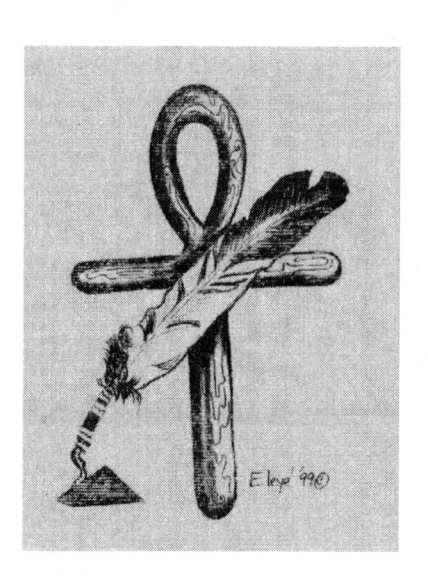

*To become distributor or for more information on this topic
Contact us at:
1-877-571-9788
or
www.blackamericanhandbook.com*

Black Americans are from the ANASAZI RACE (Ancient ones) Meaning
→ North American Algonquian

Amerindians

All Black Colleges were chartered to accept Indian Children

In 1705 all Indians were classified as "Negroes"

O Blood Type Full Blooded Indian : AB Blood Type is mixed with Indian + European

Our DNA is Mr Stronger than Largest Africans

ANKN info

1-800-571-9788
or
www.blackamericanbook.com